THE CO-LIVING REVOLUTION™

Learn how to source, design and develop Co-Living HMOs to achieve high returns and create spaces your tenants love.

STUART SCOTT

2019 UK PROPERTY DEVELOPER OF THE YEAR AND
2018 UK PROPERTY INVESTOR OF THE YEAR

ReThink

First published in Great Britain in 2022
by Rethink Press (www.rethinkpress.com)

Illustrations designed & produced by Stuart Scott

Book creative direction by Stuart Scott

Architectural photography by Richard Chivers

Lifestyle photography by Emma Cromen

THE CO-LIVING REVOLUTION™

THE CO-LIVING REVOLUTION™

THE CO-LIVING REVOLUTION™

CONTENTS _

PART FOUR _ BRAND, COMMUNITY, EXPERIENCE, & SCALE

INTRO_

What worked many years ago in property investment will no longer work now; it is a different market out there today. If you want to build a highly profitable rental portfolio, then you need to embrace new thinking and add extra skills to your toolkit.

This book is for anyone thinking of investing in houses of multiple occupation (HMOs) or upgrading their existing portfolio. I will show you how anyone, regardless of their experience, can learn to create co-living HMOs that outperform the competition and achieve high returns.

Most people tend to have a figure as their definition of financial freedom. For me, it was about replacing my old salary, which I achieved within the first twelve months of my full-time property journey using the methods I will share in this book.

Creating an additional revenue stream to complement or replace your existing income is your first objective. Even experienced developers need regular cash flow to cover overheads between each project for sale. Co-living HMOs have the potential to achieve this objective much faster than traditional buy-to-lets through greater returns.

Once you have replaced your income, the second objective is to future-proof your portfolio. You do this by constantly updating your product to ensure you always have a competitive edge in the market. The SPACES model, which we will look at in detail in Part Two of this book, will enable you to create a portfolio that attracts plenty of enquiries, achieves high rents, maximises end values and drives long-term occupancy. It doesn't matter if you are new to property or an experienced portfolio landlord; the customer has changed, so you need to adapt.

It is not all plain sailing – there will be plenty of challenges along the way. Property can be a rollercoaster ride, so as developers, we need to persevere and show resilience when facing challenges. To illustrate what I mean and help you on your journey, I will share with you my experiences – those where things went well and those when they did not. Many landlords I've worked with through my training company The Co-Living Revolution have used the models and processes outlined in this book to achieve their goals, so along with my own project case studies, I have scattered some client case studies throughout this book. They will show you the results that are possible.

Why co-living HMOs?

When they're done correctly, high-quality co-living HMOs can be a high-yielding alternative to traditional buy-to-lets and 'vanilla' HMOs. In any industry, customers are willing to spend more on a great product and an even better experience. In this book, I will cover the simple steps you can take to create a co-living HMO product that guarantees high returns and happy customers.

The HMO market in the UK is rapidly changing and becoming increasingly competitive. The customer has a lot more choice, so landlords who don't invest in their product are at risk of being hit with occupancy issues. That said, it is an exciting time to be in property right now. The changes the shared-living market is going through are providing a huge opportunity for landlords. Across the world, a wave of innovation is bringing new methodologies and approaches to the property sector.

The modern landlord is required to be an expert in customer insight, product design, customer experience and brand. That may sound daunting, but don't worry. You don't need to be an expert personally; you just need to learn and leverage from someone who is.

After more than twenty-five years in the design, technology and innovation sector, I saw a gap in the market to use the skills I had acquired to change a dated HMO industry. My wife and I were already investing in buy-to-let property as a side hobby and our strategy was simple: buy properties to which we could add maximum value and design a great end product to increase revaluation.

When I went full time into property, I needed to work on a high cash-flow strategy to replace my income. Buy-to-lets would take too long to return on my investment of both time and money, which led me to the HMO market. I saw first-hand how local HMO developers were cutting corners and doing everything on the cheap, which was giving the industry a bad reputation.

My mission became clear. I would use my skills to drive change through innovation.

Alongside my own developments, my company, The Co-Living Revolution, trains and mentors other landlords to help them build their own HMO portfolios. I am on a mission to ensure HMO landlords can replace their incomes faster, design a great product and future-proof their portfolio, and through the pages of this book, I want to extend that help to you.

As you are reading this book, I'm guessing you are interested in developing top-quality HMOs. You may have identified that you need a high cash-flow strategy and the timing is perfect for you to create your own co-living HMO product. HMOs have the potential to provide you with financial freedom while improving the lives of your customers – a true win-win – so I invite you to join the co-living movement. Together, let's shake things up, re-write the rules and create design-led properties that build thriving communities.

Here are a few of the reasons I am best placed to help you on your journey:

- My business helped pioneer the co-living movement in the UK many years ago and has inspired thousands of developers across the country.
- My projects have driven innovation, setting many of the trends now popular in the UK HMO industry.
- I am regarded as a thought leader and have been delivering keynote talks at events on the subject since 2014.

Industry awards

2018 Winner
Property Investor Of The Year

2018 Winner
HMO Deal Of The Year

This book is an overview of the models and systems I have developed through my business over many years. I haven't jumped on a bandwagon and simply added 'co-living' to standard HMOs; I have been experimenting and innovating in this area since 2014, so everything I will share is based on many years of experience. Expertise in any subject requires hard work and a lot of time.

Get the strategic edge

What is it that makes brands such as Apple and Dyson so successful in seemingly saturated markets? They have the edge and think differently, and to survive and thrive in any business today, you need that edge too.

If you're spending a lot of money on assets in the form of property, you need to be 100% sure you can fill your rooms. This requires a mindset change where tenants become your customers, properties become your product and you focus on the brand experience. This book will help you with this and give you the tools to become a more product- and customer-focused landlord.

At some point, you will unveil your new HMO product to customers and hopefully they will buy, but yours will not be the only product out there. Many other investors are looking at HMOs to fast track their financial freedom, so lots of competitors will want to tempt your customers with their alternatives. This is why you need to get ahead of the curve.

You need the edge that will enable you to create a desirable product with a queue of customers; that will help you achieve the highest returns; that will ensure you get the best valuation when you remortgage. This book is more than just a guide to creating co-living HMOs; it is the formula for getting a competitive edge in the property rental market.

Product design is all about understanding your customers' needs, identifying gaps in the market and creating new products that will deliver an amazing experience. If you create a low-quality product with a bad customer experience, your brand reputation will be affected and customers will leave. Strong brand loyalty comes from a consistently great product and experience that mean customers will prioritise and pay more for your offering.

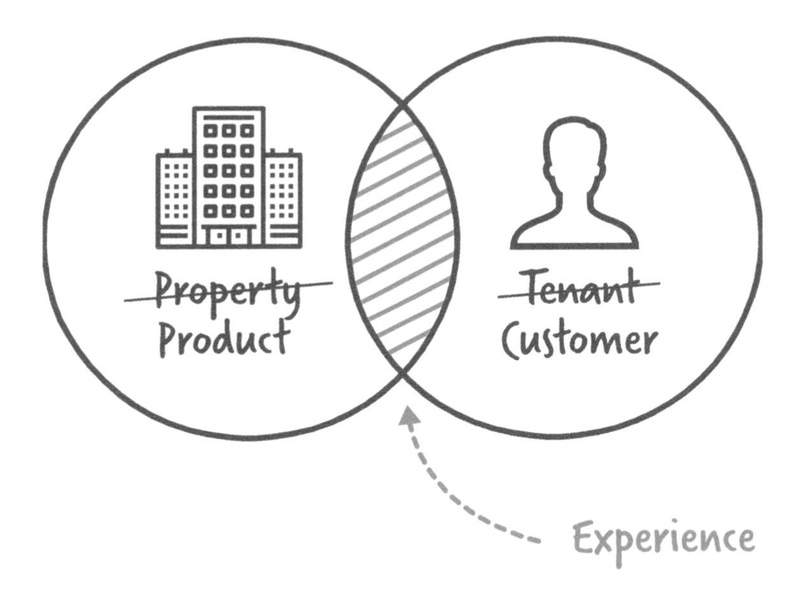

The focus on brand, product and customer experience was sadly lacking in the traditional HMO market. It's time to redefine shared living and bring new approaches to the market with the tools and systems I will be sharing in this book. Before you know it, your competitors will be looking to you for inspiration.

When a market is changing, the worst thing you can do is stand still. If you are an existing HMO landlord, what has served you for many years may no longer work moving forward. There is a huge opportunity right now to deliver a product and service that are ahead of the competition.

This book will help you to improve your offering and maximise your returns. Using the strategies we'll discuss, I have created many deals with very little money left in. You can do the same.

PART ONE _
INTRODUCING CO-LIVING HMOS

WHAT IS CO-LIVING?

Before we get started, let's have a look at what co-living is and how it differs to traditional HMOs. Like any property strategy, co-living has evolved out of existing markets based on changing customer needs and demands. Understanding where it has come from and what has driven this change will allow you to capitalise on the opportunity to create better properties.

A high-yielding strategy

Like many landlords, my wife and I started out with traditional buy-to-let properties, otherwise known as single lets. Wanting to invest some of our savings into appreciating assets that could provide an additional income for us, we reconfigured the properties to add bedrooms, modernised the finish and rented them out via local letting agents.

I don't mind admitting we rolled up our sleeves and got stuck in to deliver the refurbishments, but the real revelation came when our letting agents sent us the rent minus their fees. The amount we received effectively gave us a secondary income stream beyond our day jobs and it felt amazing. Every month without fail, rental money continued to hit our bank account.

Given how hard we were working every day for our salary, it was an amazing feeling to receive a monthly profit on an asset that was also increasing in value each year. After the success of our first buy-to-let, we naturally considered how we could finance buying more.

Once we completed each single-let project, we remortgaged and refinanced a small amount of the money – we call this process recycling. This uplift was possible through buying at the right price, modernisation and adding bedrooms, the end goal being to achieve a revaluation significantly higher than our total project spend. The distance between these two numbers dictated our ability to recycle more cash and finance further projects.

In many cases, we found we were leaving a fair amount of our funds in the deal, which raised the issue of our money running out. Single lets were starting to look like a capital-intensive strategy for the amount of rental returns.

After developing a number of single-let properties, we realised it might be possible to replace our incomes entirely via a buy-to-let portfolio, but it dawned on us that we would need a large number of single lets to achieve this. How could we possibly finance that many property purchases? We needed to find a way to achieve much higher rental returns for our capital invested. It was this search that led us to the world of HMOs.

The term HMO is a property rented by the room. Tenants have access to shared facilities such as kitchens, lounges, bathrooms and gardens. Unlike traditional single-let properties, HMOs provide multiple streams of income within one asset as they are rented to multiple tenants, creating much greater cash flow and profit. While a traditional single let yields no income when it's empty, an HMO keeps cash flowing from all its other rooms even when one tenant leaves. As a landlord, you have more resilience to market conditions with an HMO.

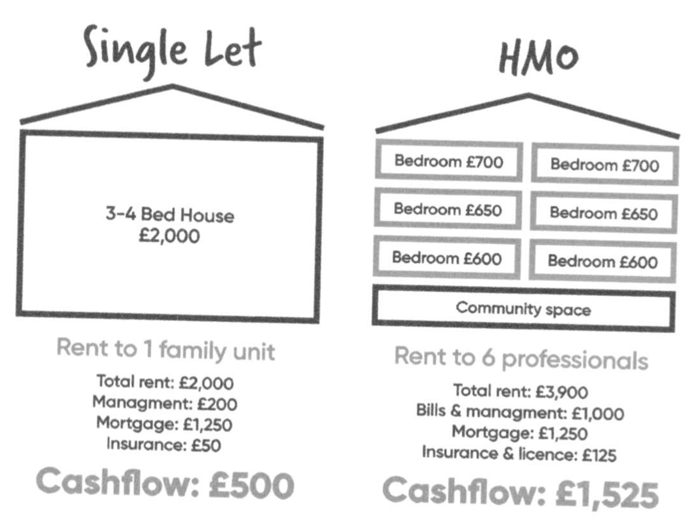

Although the numbers will change based on different projects, you can expect to see a significant increase by renting multiple rooms over single lets.

It was like a lightbulb turning on when we realised that HMOs could help us replace our income faster than single lets. HMOs were the perfect step up from traditional buy-to-let into higher-yielding alternatives. Given the rather low standard of other landlords' HMOs, we could see there was a huge opportunity to create a high-quality portfolio with a focus on design and experience.

Single Let vs HMOs
Replace your income faster
Target: £50,000 / £4,166 per month

Fewer high-yielding HMO properties are required to achieve income goals compared to lower-yielding single lets.

Shared living is nothing new

Humans have lived together for thousands of years. In medieval times, people shared resources and even sleeping accommodation.[1] Most homes were shared by friends and extended family; single-family households were uncommon across most of the world.

In the nineteenth and twentieth century, boarding houses, with their separate sleeping accommodation, but communal meals, housekeeping and community events, paved the way towards more independent living. During the Industrial Revolution, the United States and Europe saw a rise of boarding houses and people lodging with families as increasing numbers migrated towards areas of employment. These same boarding houses then provided much-needed accommodation during the world wars.[2]

The recent co-living trend started in the United States, inspired by the 'hacker houses' in Silicon Valley.[3] This new market provides opportunities for micro-living in overpriced cities across the US. The real-estate market is one of the few big markets untapped by the technology giants, which has led to a wave of entrepreneurs setting up co-living companies such as Common,[4] Habyt,[5] The Collective,[6] Bungalow,[7] CoHabs[8] and Zoku.[9] These companies have many similarities to technology start-ups, with a strong focus on product innovation and design while leading with customer experience.

We are now seeing these companies enter the UK and European markets with substantial funding behind them. The co-living trend has also been gaining traction in Asia Pacific, particularly in markets like Hong Kong, China and India, driven by housing affordability and an increase in urban population.[10]

The evolution of the HMO into co-living

All products go through a natural evolution and the property industry is no different. Just as bedsits went out of fashion many years ago, the HMO has also gone through a similar evolutionary change.

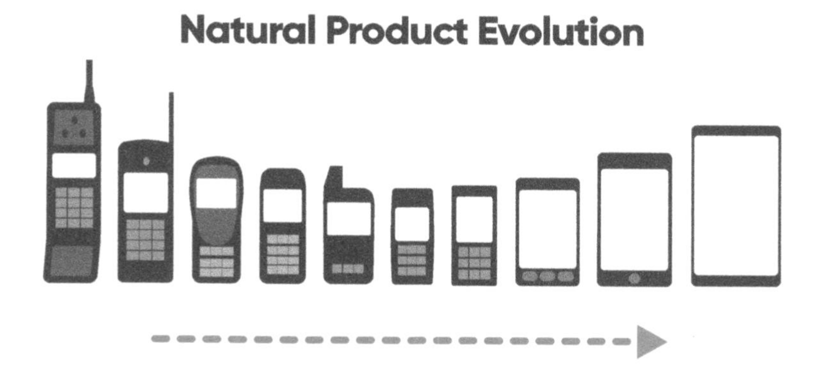

A good example of product evolution is the mobile phone. What started as a simple communication device is now a powerful computer integrated to all our social channels. Many of the changes during the phone's evolution have been driven by a mix of customer needs, new technology and improved manufacturing, and these same factors apply to the HMO market. The customer has changed, technology has advanced and the product has evolved.

A lot of people talk about saturation in the HMO market, but innovative products are not affected by saturation in the same way as vanilla products. The mobile phone market was saturated with competitors offering similar products, then along came Apple with a ground-breaking touchscreen technology and user experience. This disruption to the market caused a step change where competitors rushed to evolve their products to keep up. As soon as the customer has more choice and access to a better experience in any market, everyone has to raise their game or risk falling behind.

UK HMO licensing and planning permission

Prior to the rise of co-living, the UK already had an established shared-living market under the definition of HMO which arose from the Housing Act 1985. This act first defined an HMO as 'a house which is occupied by persons who do not form a single household'.[11] As people living in an HMO do not come from the same family, they are deemed as separate households.

There is currently no specific planning class for co-living HMOs with fewer than fifty rooms, which means that any planning application for co-living is basically an HMO planning application. If you think of co-living as an evolution of the HMO, then this will be easier to remember. This is one of the reasons I use the term co-living HMOs instead of just co-living.

The definition of HMO from the UK's GOV website is:

> 'Your home is a house in multiple occupation (HMO) if both of the following apply: at least three tenants live there, forming more than one household, [and they] share toilet, bathroom or kitchen facilities with other tenants.'[12]

If your property meets these criteria, you will need a licence for HMOs.

HMO licences make sure the landlord meets certain standards on fire safety, room sizes, amenities and health and safety. It is surprising that so many landlords complain about licences when the objective is to ensure their tenants are safe. You can contact your local HMO officer or download a copy of the HMO standards via your local council's website. These standards will list out any requirements that you will need to add to your works, such as fire doors, grade of fire alarm, door closers, emergency lighting, rooms sizes, locked cupboards and window restrictors.

A key thing to remember is that licensing and planning permission are two different things. Now you would think that the two departments talk together, but that's not usually the case. It is possible for you to get a licence for an HMO, but still be in breach of planning permission. In many areas, you can change a C3 residential house (used by one household) into a C4 HMO (a small, shared house containing between three and six unrelated tenants) using permitted development (PD). In this instance, you don't need planning permission, but you will need to get a HMO licence and building control sign off.

If you are in an area covered by an Article 4 direction – used by councils to restrict the spread and density of HMOs – then you will need to submit a full planning application. When you're looking at any new sites or potential locations, always check for restrictions such as Article 4 or conservation area.

HMOs for seven or more tenants come under a class called sui generis. These larger HMOs require full planning permission, so I advise you to seek the help of a local planning consultant so that you can assess the viability of potential sites.

If you're buying an existing sui generis HMO, always confirm that it has the correct planning permissions or look to obtain a certificate of lawfulness, but I recommend starting by converting PD C3 houses to C4 HMOs for up to six people. This is a good low-risk foundation for your high-yield portfolio. Once you have a few co-living HMO projects under your belt, then you can move on to a range of larger sites.

There is a whole range of building types suitable for conversion into co-living HMOs, dependent on your level of experience and the stage of your property journey. Here are a few to consider:

- **Mini-mos.** These are small houses and apartments with two to four bedrooms. Unless you are in an Article 4 area, these conversions to HMO would be under PD.
- **Houses of up to six unrelated people (C4).** This is one of the most popular strategies as the cash flow is high. Assuming you are not in an Article 4 area, C4 HMOs can be converted under PD.
- **Sui generis HMOs of seven+ people.** As you evolve your property search, you may view larger properties with scope for further rooms. When your property houses seven or more unrelated people, you will need to put in full planning permission for conversion from residential to sui generis HMO.
- **Commercial conversion to large sui generis HMO.** If the property you are converting was originally used under a commercial class such as retail or office, the same rules apply as for sui generis HMOs. The upside is that there is less competition in this space as many investors stick to PD schemes.
- **Commercial conversion to mixed-use HMOs, single lets and commercial.** This is a more advanced strategy where you can utilise prior approvals to create a mixed scheme, blending HMOs, sui generis HMOs, single lets and small commercial units. Certain sites will lend themselves to a mixed scheme rather than a large HMO, which may be more positively received by the local planning department.
- **Commercial conversion to clusters of HMOs.** This is similar to the previous strategy, but without any commercial or single lets, thus providing multiple HMOs in the same building. Given that tenants often want to live in small communities where they get to know each other, the 'cluster' approach can provide a great way to achieve a high density of occupation without creating an impersonal oversized HMO.
- **Build to rent.** If you are even more adventurous, you may look at land for sale with the purpose of building from the ground up. I would recommend you seek expert advice before embarking on this option.

The three pillars of co-living

Unlike traditional HMOs, co-living has an emphasis on building an engaged community and supporting a healthy social lifestyle. When you combine this with the significant cost savings for both the tenants and the landlords, you can see why so many people are embracing this new form of shared living.

The diagram shows the three pillars that make up modern co-living.

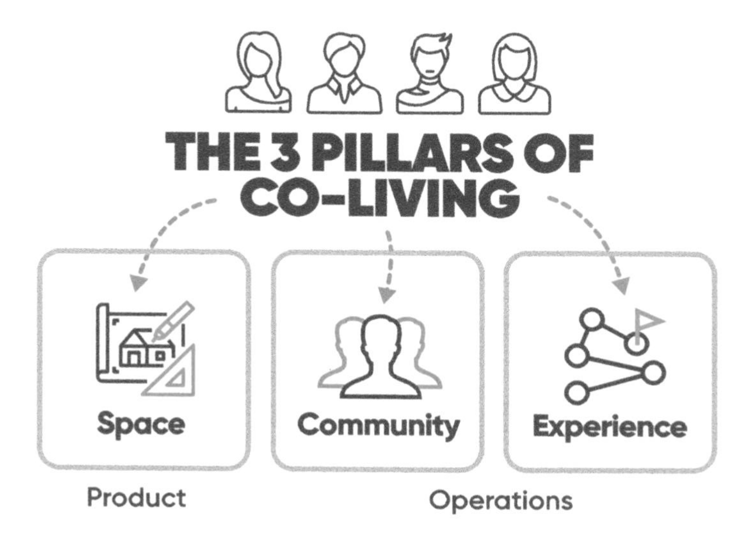

When combined, these three pillars provide the ultimate in co-living: a space, social community and brand experience that make people feel so great, they recommend it to their friends.

Space. Design and build spaces that are a pleasure for your customers to live in and environments for them to socialise in, together with a range of spaces for collaboration across work and play.

Community. Co-living has an emphasis on building an engaged community, bringing housemates together and enabling them to form better bonds and relationships.

CO-LIVING
SPACES

Experience. There is no point creating a great space and community if the overall service is bad. If you create an awesome brand experience, your customers will become fans.

Understand your customer

Early on in your co-living HMO journey, you will need to decide who your target market is. I always wanted to focus on the professional end of the market; one of the reasons I got into developing shared-living properties was the feedback I got from my former employees who complained about the standard of accommodation in the area. This stuck with me for many years until I came into property developing full time. Then I could focus on solving that problem.

The models in this book are applicable to both the student and the professional markets. I have mentored landlords over the years who have used these models to create the best student accommodation in their area.

How do you service your target market? Let's look at the needs of the different generations in the workforce. Millennials and Generation Z have grown up with access to the internet and technology and, on the whole, smartphones and social media too. Generation Z have never experienced anything other than high bandwidth, on-demand TV and always-on connectivity. They and Millennials want ultra-fast wi-fi, the latest technology, convenience, comfort and a social lifestyle, and they are happy to pay extra for an experience that provides this.

As working habits change, living spaces will need to adapt to meet the demands of today's digital nomads and semi-remote workers. With the increasing popularity of working from home, Generation X will also demand greater access to technology, along with the large bedrooms, plenty of room for storage, wide range of facilities and access to outdoor spaces that my company's research has identified this age group prefers. Later in the book, I will share with you how to create co-working spaces to adapt to this changing demand.

Addressing loneliness and social isolation

I have lost track of the number of times I have spoken to a new customer who tells me their story of living in a one-bedroom flat or studio and feeling lonely. They value their private space but crave social interaction.

I lived in HMOs as I grew up in Brighton, forging lifelong friendships and a strong social circle that I treasure to this day. When I got home from a hard day of work, I had the option whether to socialise or not. My housemates and I would often take it in turns to cook, then we would eat together, enjoy film nights, host barbecues or play board games. If I didn't feel like joining in, I had the option of the privacy of my room, but I never needed to feel alone.

Convenience and value for money

Depending on the customer's stage of life, personal situation and financial position, they will evaluate co-living HMOs alongside self-contained options such as studios and apartments. Young working professionals who may be new to the area are likely to be looking to meet people and make friends while they climb the corporate ladder. At this stage, customers want a service that will make their lives simple. Studios and apartments can be expensive not only in terms of money, but also in terms of the time it takes to deal with utilities and bills and keep the place clean.

A recent study from Built Asset Management found a 312% increase in renters ditching single-let apartments in favour of co-living HMOs.[13] They gave value for money and avoiding isolation as their top reasons for this decision.

Eventually, working professionals will require more space and access to different facilities such as outside areas and co-working. At some point, they may settle down with a partner, move city or decide to go off travelling, for example. Although you may think this is the end of that particular customer journey, in my experience, many return if their circumstances change.

You may also have older customers who are single, new to the area or recently divorced. Unlike traditional HMOs, co-living HMOs offer an attractive alternative to potentially expensive single-let accommodation for this group of people. They tend to look for larger rooms, better facilities and a more mature community (ie not a party house).

Summary

In this chapter, we have covered the background of co-living HMOs and why they have evolved in line with changing customer needs. We have discussed the range of buildings suitable for co-living HMOs and explored what makes this accommodation option so popular.

Co-living HMOs provide a sustainable way for people to share resources and live in urban areas. In the United Kingdom, we live on an island with a finite supply of land and a growing population, which requires creative solutions. Cities of the distant future will be vastly different to anything we can imagine today, but you only need to look at Manhattan to see how a small area has already adapted to house the mass of people who live and work there.

In the next chapter, I will provide an overview of the SPACES model: the blueprint for my success in the world of the co-living HMO. The rest of the book will then cover each of the six steps of SPACES – strategy, product, attraction, community, experience, scale – in fine detail.

The SPACES model has been the blueprint for the property success I have enjoyed. In fact, I would go as far as to say it underpins everything we do.

Examples of our co-living HMO social spaces

SPACES

THE SIX-STEP SPACES MODEL

The SPACES model is the amalgamation of over twenty-five years' experience in human-centred design and innovation – a quest to create amazing products and systems to delight the user and improve people's lives. We have carefully moulded the golden nuggets from that experience into six easy-to-follow steps to create desirable co-living HMOs. You don't need to come from a creative background to follow this model; you just need to be able to embrace new thinking and adapt to change.

With the SPACES model, you will learn the **strategies** you'll require to source your own co-living HMO sites. You'll discover how to create the best **product** on the market and **attract** customers, nurture a **community**, provide a great **experience** and **scale** your property business. If you follow this simple model, you will be able to create a thriving property business that is constantly ahead of the curve.

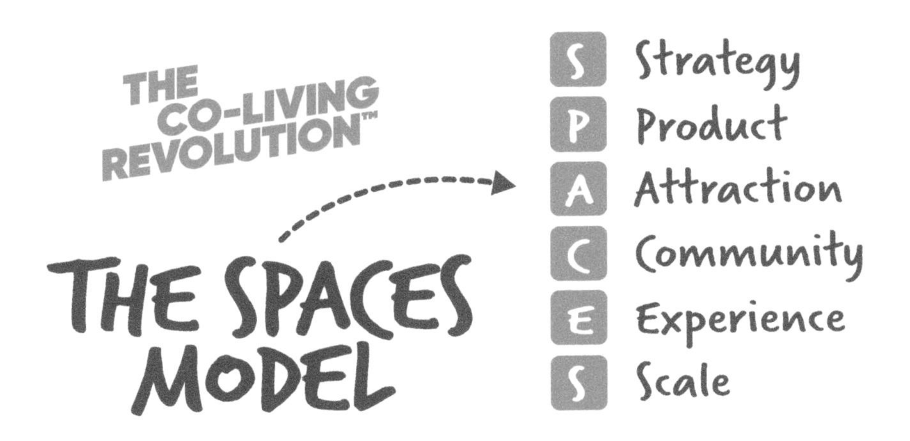

Before we move on to Part Two, 'Strategy', let's enjoy an overview of each of the six steps of the SPACES model.

Strategy

Having a solid strategy is key to maintaining momentum towards your goals. Without it, you will lack clarity and will not feel confident enough to take action. Part Two will show you how to be highly strategic to take your co-living HMO business to the next level.

I break strategy into five key stages:

- **Foundations and the buy, refurbish, refinance and rent (BRRR) model** – the foundations to ensure you build a successful property business. Make your finances go further and leave less money tied up in your deals.
- **Deal analysis, criteria and funding** – define your criteria, utilise spreadsheets, assess key costs and use scheme design and valuations to help you stack deals more efficiently. Learn how to fund your co-living HMO projects and work with private investors and small self-administered scheme (SASS) pension funding.
- **Find your investment area** – learn how to discover your target investment areas, gather key data, shortlist the best locations and find your patches.
- **Types of building conversion** – explore a range of property opportunities from PD through to full planning permission and commercial conversions.
- **Methods and techniques** – learn how to ensure you are continually sourcing new property opportunities and managing the deal flow (pipeline).

Product

Once you have your strategy in place, the next thing to think about is the product you are going to be offering to customers. This is where you deep dive into customer insight to design an irresistible product – the same process Apple uses to create a queue of customers for its new releases.[14]

As a landlord and developer, you need to design and build products that are valuable and enjoyable for the end user. You are developing a product for customers (tenants) and your properties are your product line. Like any good product designer, you need to continually adapt and evolve to stay ahead of the curve. The Space Design Blueprint, which we will look at in Chapter 10, is a simple reference model to deliver co-living HMOs that are always one step ahead. Use this as your secret weapon to get the edge.

Attraction

Once you have your strategy and product sorted, the next thing you need to think about is how to attract your ideal customer, and this means brand and marketing. Some of you may be thinking that you don't need to build a brand if you're planning to have your sites managed by an agent. My own brand and marketing have attracted millions of pounds' worth of private investment, created joint venture (JV) opportunities and provided a constant stream of customer enquiries. Need I say any more?

I cut my teeth working in brand, marketing and ad agencies. I then went on to build my own creative agency and product-design company, and have used my experience to create the Build a Brand model which we will cover in Chapter 12. Even if you don't know anything about brand or marketing, this simple system will ensure you have a visible property brand, digital presence and ongoing marketing strategy to attract new leads and opportunities.

Community

Building a community is one of the three pillars of co-living we looked at in the previous chapter. Community is a key reason co-living HMOs are so attractive to customers looking for a social lifestyle. If you can help nurture a community in your properties, this will have a direct impact on long-term occupancy levels.

In this part of the book, we are going to cover the importance of an onboarding process, the role of community managers, organising events and partnerships, interconnected communities, shared-interest groups and finding the right housemates.

Experience

There is no point getting this far, with a sound strategy, a great product, a supercharged marketing engine and the plans in place for a thriving community, if no one enjoys the overall experience. I'm sure we can all think of times when we have engaged with a brand and got an awful customer service.

This step of SPACES is about shifting your mindset away from product to the wider customer experience. Creating a great product is important, but without an even better customer experience, it will fall short. It is the time to take your killer product and put a rocket under it to give you a huge market advantage.

Scale

The time will come when you have a sound strategy, a great product, a marketing engine, a growing community and happy customers. Wouldn't it be great if that was 'job done'? Unfortunately, there's more. You now need to think about how to scale your business to the next level.

The team, the systems and the processes that may have worked for one project will need to change if you're to build a successful co-living HMO business. You may have rolled up your sleeves and done everything yourself to get started, but now you need to think about how to manage simultaneous property developments.

As you scale your portfolio, you will start to see the fruits of your hard work financially. Before you know it, your financial targets will be in sight. In this part, covering the final step of SPACES, I will show you the methods I have used to scale our business and how to create your own repeatable blueprint.

Summary

In this chapter, I have introduced you to the six steps of the SPACES model – strategy, product, attraction, community, experience and scale. No one step is more important than the others; they are all essential to ensure you stand out in the world of co-living HMOs, but you do need to work on them in order. There's no gain from building a memorable customer experience if you have no product for the customers to enjoy, and you won't scale far without the preceding five steps in place.

Now you know what co-living HMOs are, why they are such a win-win option for both landlords and their customers, and the model to use to build a successful property portfolio and achieve financial independence, you're ready to start your journey in Part Two. It's time to build your strategy.

PART TWO _
STRATEGY

BUILDING YOUR FOUNDATIONS

To achieve your goals, you need to be clear on your strategy. If you're not clear on this, you may be heading in the wrong direction and wasting time on the wrong things.

As developers, we constantly evolve year on year as we invest in our knowledge and education. I always refer to the two stages we go through as property investors, the first being personally as developers and the second being the output we create, otherwise known as the product. This 'Strategy' part of the book is all about the first step of the SPACES model, which helps you become a better developer and enables you to spot opportunities and achieve high returns.

This is the same five step strategy system we teach landlords on our Co-Living Mastermind programme, and we are going to give you a high level view of all five stages so that you can get started on your co-living HMO journey.

Focus on cash flow first

If you are just starting out, you obviously need to create cash flow quickly to replace your income and this must take priority. You may decide to invest in cheap areas with little competition to build the cash flow and hit your targets; there is no right or wrong here. The most important thing is to make whatever you decide to do part of a wider strategy and vision for your overall portfolio.

A portfolio should be about both short- and long-term performance. I buy assets in good, well-connected central areas that have data to support capital growth and strong rental demand. I then add huge value, maximise rents and hold them for the long term – I like to have a blend of high cash flow and capital appreciation. This approach allows me to refinance capital lump sums in the future, giving me multiple revenue streams from the same assets.

THE 5 STEP STRATEGY MODEL

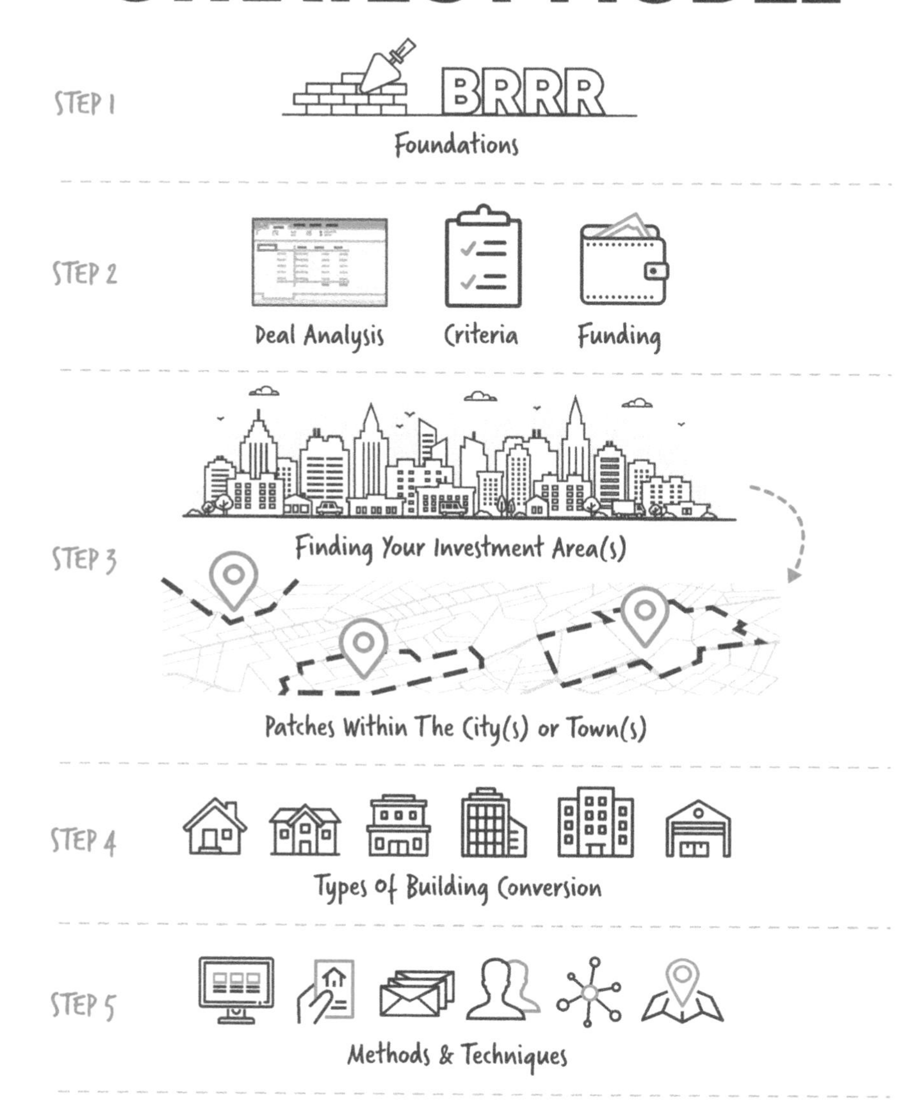

As part of your strategy, you will need to decide whether to hold properties to build up cash-flow income or sell (flip) them to make lump sums. If you are at the start of your co-living HMO journey, chances are your focus will be on replacing your income with cash flow. Holding on to properties will help you achieve your targets and, in time, build equity through adding value and capital appreciation.

The question of hold vs flip also depends on what type of deals you find and where you are located. If you are located in an expensive area, you will need a strategy for the funds you leave in every deal as you probably won't be able to recycle every penny. By adding at least one flip per year into your pipeline, you will create lump sums of capital that will help mitigate this issue.

Personal name or limited company

Before you start to purchase sites for conversion to co-living HMOS, you will need to decide if you are buying in your own name or in the name of a limited company. This depends on your personal financial situation and any other earnings you have.

I have properties both in my personal name and across various limited companies. Limited companies pay corporation tax rather than income tax, while personally, you can earn up to £50,000 before your income tax jumps from 20% to a whopping 40%. If you have current earnings or a salary and you add rental income on top of this, it may tip you into the 40% band.

To help mitigate this risk, more and more landlords are setting up a limited company when buying rental property, but the changes to mortgage interest tax relief only affect private and individual landlords and are not applicable to limited companies. I would recommend speaking to an accountant about your plans for property so that you can put the most tax-efficient approach in place.

Build your co-living HMO power team

Regardless of whether you are working on your first co-living HMO or have a few projects under your belt, you will need a good power team around you. Initially, many of your team members will be external to your business, such as freelancers and tradespeople, but as you scale, you may employ people on either a fixed contract, part-time or full-time basis.

At the start of your property journey, your team will include mortgage brokers, architects, accountants, bookkeepers, builders, surveyors and letting agents. As you progress into larger and more complex projects, your team will expand to include planning consultants, party wall surveyors, project managers, tax consultants and capital allowance consultants.

Having a good mentor on your power team will fast track your progress and support you to achieve your goals. You can leverage a mentor's knowledge to minimise mistakes and provide accountability to keep you on track.

I recommend you create a central spreadsheet which lists your power team. Think of this as your roster of contacts. Every year, it is a good idea to add new contacts to your roster so that if you get let down by a supplier, you have alternatives to choose from.

The way people work has changed. I have embraced a mixture of flexible semi-remote working powered by cloud-based software. There are some amazing project-management tools and video-conferencing technologies out there, meaning you can tap into an army of highly talented people looking for flexible work.

Ten ways to add value to your developments

One of the key strategies when you're building your portfolio is to add value to every project you work on. By taking this approach, you will achieve high valuations, receive high income and recycle more of your funds. As serial renovators, adding value was fundamental to all our projects.

One of the key skills to master is spotting opportunities to add value that others miss. This is the difference between the numbers on a deal working or not. All of our projects follow this simple foundation for adding value:

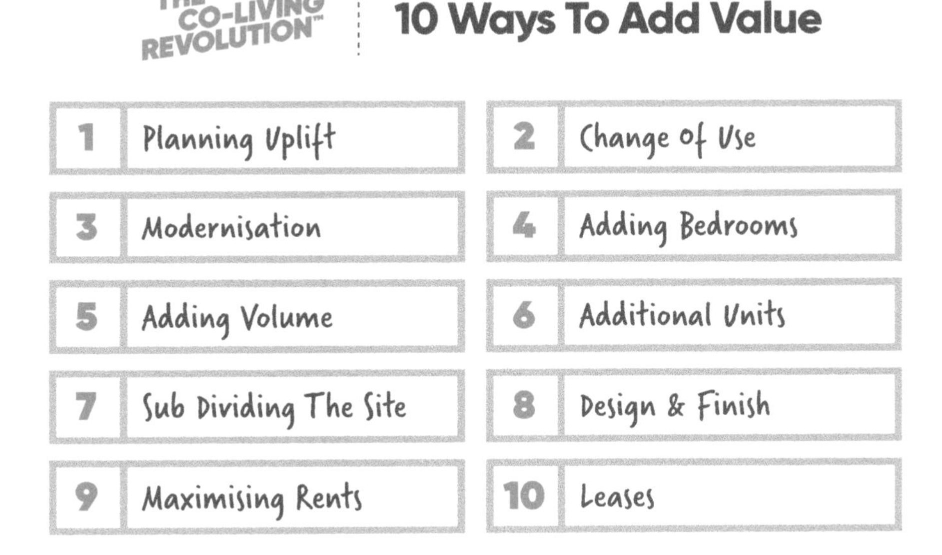

The BRRR model

If you want to build a property portfolio to replace your income, you need a strategy that will make your funds go as far as possible. Property development is capital intensive so you will run out of money after a certain number of projects. Dependent on the area of the country you live in, you may run out of funds sooner than you anticipate if the property and work cost more than you budgeted for.

The BRRR model is a great way to recycle some of your initial funds, based on a new higher valuation. The model is split across four stages:

1. **Buy:** target, negotiate and buy the right property at the right price
2. **Refurbish:** add value through development to achieve a high-end valuation

3. **Refinance:** remortgage the property based on the new valuation, releasing a portion of funds back to yourself
4. **Rent:** maximise rental income and occupancy levels through investing in a design-led product and great customer experience

As I operate in an expensive area, I do not have any alternative but to buy well and add maximum value to enable the recycling of funds. If I did not do this, I would be leaving a lot of money in every project.

As a developer, you have to have a strategy to access the funds left in your properties. Without it, you will run out of money quickly. We have covered a number of techniques for recycling your funds in this chapter, but I can't stress enough how important it is to buy at the right price and add value to a project. This is one of the greatest skills you can learn when assessing new deals.

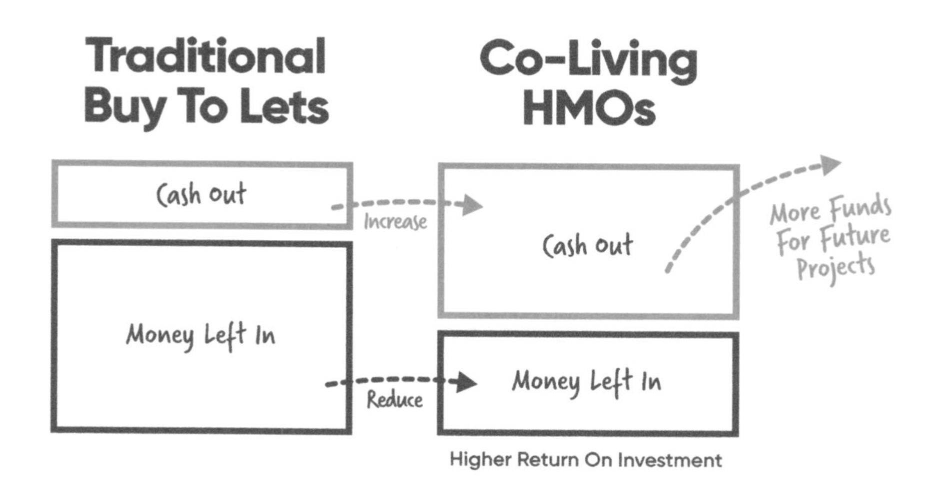

CASE STUDY

BRRR Model C3 Residential to C4 Co-Living HMO

This case study involves a probate property which required a complete renovation ('back to brick', as we call it).; it was the worst house on the best road in an area of strong capital appreciation. As I always do, I travelled to view the site when the agent called me and met the seller at the property. He wanted the sale to be quick and appreciated how selling to a local developer could enable this, regardless of the property's run-down condition and the works required.

Using the ten ways to add value I shared earlier, I increased the end valuation by modernising the property, reconfiguring the layout, putting in a loft conversion and adding more rooms. Under PD, I converted a three-bedroom house into a six-bedroom co-living HMO which achieved high rents and demand. I then created a 'valuer pack' for the bank surveyor to share the level of works I'd completed on the property and ensure the best possible refinance deal.

Here's a summary of the deal:

- Property sourced through local agent.
- Purchase price £372,500. Refurb and fit out costs approximately £118,000.
- Post-refinance mortgage 75% loan to value (LTV) in area of strong capital appreciation. Monthly mortgage and bills £2,304.
- Rented out as a six-bedroom co-living HMO with a monthly income of £4,230 (£50,760 annual).
- Achieved a bricks-and-mortar revaluation of £600,000.
- Total monthly profit of £1,925 (£23,102 annually), giving a return on investment (ROI) of 29%.
- Recycled approximately 70% of original funds after refinance.

Although I could have extended at the rear of the property, I decided against doing this in case the property was ever turned into a family house again. This approach left the property with multiple exits, should they be needed in the future.

In this example, I bought at a good price in a great location and added significant value. The project allowed me to recycle around 70% of my original funds and use this money on further projects.

LIVE
MORE
WORRY
LESS

CASSETTELORD

Summary

In this chapter, we have looked at the foundations of your strategy. With anything you build, be it a business or a property, it's essential to have strong foundations in place before you begin. There's no better way to supercharge your foundations than with a great power team.

Wherever you are on your property-development journey, cash flow will remain a key consideration. We have looked at the ways to maximise the return you get from your investments, both in terms of rental income and appreciation in value of the property itself. The ten ways to add value to your developments and the BRRR model will stand you in good stead to achieve financial freedom, far sooner than you expect.

We're now ready to move on to stage two of the Strategy: Deal Analysis.

Find out how Yolande secured her first property to convert into a co-living HMO. Yolande identified a building perfect to add value and extra rooms. With the knowledge she gained through The Co-Living Mastermind™, she is now confidently working with builders to deliver her first co-living HMO.

To watch the full video visit
www.theco-livingrevolution.co.uk/mastermind

DEAL ANALYSIS

With the foundations of your strategy in place, it's time to turn your attention to the property deals available to you. The first thing you need to do is assess the viability of any property leads you identify, arming yourself with the information you need to make an educated decision. This chapter will take you through each stage of deal analysis, from spreadsheets and criteria through to figures, schemes and funding.

Being able to assess new leads in your deal pipeline is a vital skill for a developer and landlord. This is an area with potential 'blockers', so it is good to invest some time to get a solid process in place. Then one of the best ways to smash these blockers is to 'learn by doing' and start stacking deals.

Before you start any deal analysis, you will need some information upfront to help you assess the site for development. When I spot a new lead, this is the information I gather:

- Floorplans with room measurements or volumes
- Vendor's (seller's) circumstances and reason for selling
- Current use class and planning history on the site or within the road
- Any restrictions such as Article 4, conservation or title restrictions
- Whether the property is on the open market yet or if the vendor is looking for a quick sale

Armed with this information, you will be able to analyse the potential opportunity and returns available more accurately.

HMO deal-stacking spreadsheet

Love them or hate them, spreadsheets are an essential tool for deal analysis. You need to centralise all the numbers to work out if a deal meets your criteria. There are two main options for you: Excel or Google Sheets. Personally, I use Google Sheets hosted on the cloud as part of my Google suite of tools so multiple people can collaborate on the same document at the same time. This is great for online Zoom sessions, or even when we're speaking over the phone.

Once you have chosen your platform, you will need to build a spreadsheet that factors in all the buying costs of the property deal you're considering. Here are some top tips on evaluating deals with spreadsheets:

- Double check all cell formulas used throughout the spreadsheet
- Account for all the costs, eg legals, surveys, professional fees, finance purchase costs, refurbishment, furniture and fixings, stamp duty, deposit etc
- Make sure you factor in any holding costs (for the period between purchase and rental), such as monthly mortgage payments, utilities and any investor interest
- Research end values and achievable rents, adding links to relevant comparables
- If a deal does not stack, reduce the purchase price until you meet your target ROI and consider putting an offer on the table rather than walking away

Decide on your criteria

When I work with landlords, I get them to identify their criteria early on so that they can assess and act upon new leads quickly. Not being clear on your criteria is an example of the blockers that stop you from having the confidence to act on any new leads.

Have a think about what you need to achieve from each property to replace your income. There are three key criteria I would recommend you start with. You will need to balance up each deal based on all three of these.

The first criteria is your minimum ROI – this is the return that funds invested in the deal will make based on the valuation and annual cash flow the property will create. If you are planning to use the BRRR model, this will be the ROI on your funds left in the deal after refinance.

The second key criteria is minimum cash flow. What is the lowest monthly or annual cash flow that you would be happy with once the property is rented out, cash flow being your profit after running costs such as mortgages, insurances, bills etc?

The third key criteria is the amount of funds left in the deal. Each deal will have a different level of your original funds left in post refinance.

Calculate rental estimations and end value

As part of your deal analysis, you will need to assess likely rental income and potential property end value. Never overestimate these to make the deal work; in fact, it's best to be pessimistic on these numbers to build some stress testing into the analysis.

For rental value, I would recommend using SpareRoom to gather competitor research and information on comparable high-quality rooms. I use the technique of modelling my rental figures on comparables, and then looking to outperform the numbers.

For property end values, often referred to as gross development value (GDV), I use a number of methods to cross check the potential figure:

- Free listing portals such as sold prices on Rightmove and Zoopla
- Online property software tools (see the bonus content sections for recommendations)
- Speaking to landlords at local property networking events to find out end values they've achieved
- Searching Facebook property groups by location to look for any deal posts listing valuations, rents and key numbers

When you're assessing the potential end value of your co-living HMO, its type of valuation will depend on its number of rooms and if it is part of a larger mixed scheme. There are two main types of HMO valuations you will be utilising as you grow your portfolio. One is a bricks-and-mortar valuation, and the other is an investment valuation.

Most HMOs up to six bedrooms will be valued on a bricks-and-mortar basis, meaning that the valuer will look to other recent sold-price comparables nearby. If you are developing sui generis HMOs or mixed-use sites, then the building(s) will be valued on a yield-based multiplier of the rental income. This can be a good technique to achieve higher valuations than bricks and mortar in certain locations. Investment valuations can also be a good way to recycle more funds on larger projects.

Estimate the cost of refurbishment works

When stacking your potential leads, you are going to need to assess the cost of refurbishment works. This depends entirely on the type of project you undertake. For example, are you converting a loft? Extending on the ground floor? Changing from commercial to residential? Is the building in good condition or in need of complete renovation?

If you're just starting out, you will need to use estimates before you have more accurate builders' quotes. It is advisable to allow a high per square metre (sqm) rate until you have more accurate pricing from your chosen contractor. Given fluctuating materials costs, this will build in some contingency for you.

Once you have a few co-living HMOs under your belt, you can calculate what each project cost you per sqm to refurbish and fit out. If you are planning to buy similar properties in a comparable area, this will provide accurate data to use as an estimate in your deal spreadsheets.

A useful tip on calculating your refurbs is to remember to separate your fit-out cost from the core refurbishment. You core refurbishment is the cost to convert your property and take it to a painted finish. Your fit out is the cost to add all your appliances, furniture, lighting and bespoke interior items.

Model schemes and exits

A hot new lead has hit your desk (cue celebration music) and you have run some numbers in your deal spreadsheet. The next step is to model a number of possible schemes (layouts) for the site. Even though you may have a preferred option in mind, it is worth taking a step back and assessing every possible avenue.

When you're looking at scheme models for your property deal, they will fall into one of three categories:

- **No planning required.** This is what you can achieve from the building/site with no planning permission or by utilising PD. For example, if you're converting a three-bedroom house into a six-bedroom HMO in a non-Article 4 area, this is covered by PD. A mixed-use site where you retain the commercial unit on the ground floor while converting existing residential maisonettes above it into a HMO also comes under PD.
- **Prior approval scheme.** This covers commercial buildings or mixed-use sites converted or part converted into residential via prior approval. You may source a mixed-use site with existing residential accommodation above that you could convert into a small HMO via PD, but you will need to do the conversion of the ground floor into residential apartments via Class MA.
- **Full planning scheme.** To maximise the scope of the site, you can use full planning applications for either change of use, extensions or building entirely new units. I often submit both prior approval and full planning on sites, so that the prior approval becomes a fall-back option.

When you're assessing deals, it is worth factoring in alternative future exits. Could the site be converted to another use? Is there the potential for more ambitious planning years down the road?

Fund your co-living HMO deals

Once you have located, assessed and secured a new property, the next stage is to fund your deal. Unless you are buying for cash, I'm going to assume you are planning to take out a mortgage during the build of your co-living HMO project, so having a good mortgage broker on your power team is essential as you will rely on them to review the whole of market for the best deals. It's not always the interest rate you need to consider; there are many other fees to be assessed against each lender.

Once you have a mortgage product lined up, you will be able to combine this funding with either your own money or investor money to finance the whole deal. Adding value and refinancing allows you to recycle a proportion of the funds to repay investors and work on further projects.

In addition to first-charge lending (this is the primary lender who will fund the purchase and take a legal charge on the property), you may be able to access development finance where the lender will fund the refurbishment works. Working with a whole-of-market mortgage broker with access to both residential and commercial products will give you every option for purchase and refinance. At an early stage, explain to your broker what works you are planning and what the purpose of the finished property will be.

The level of works and type of project will dictate the most suitable mortgage product. If the building is un-mortgageable or you are planning extensive works, then you will need to look at more expensive bridging-style products. Your broker will be able to work with you to find the most suitable product.

Work with investors, SASS pensions and JV partners

It doesn't matter how much money you have, you will eventually run out of funds as you grow your portfolio. If you are planning to scale in a reasonably short period of time, then you will need to work with investors to achieve this. I blend my own money along with investor funds to finance my co-living HMO projects.

As a landlord, you need to build the skill of working with investors early on in your journey. Avoiding this option until you need money is leaving it too late; you can't fast track the process. You need to build credibility and trust, which is an organic process, so the earlier you start, the better.

Investors are all around you. How many people do you know who have funds sitting in the bank, gaining almost no interest at all? However, most people are not comfortable talking about money with potential investors. The key thing to remember here is that you are not asking them for money; you are simply offering them an opportunity.

Sometimes, people think that investors are only interested in the highest return. What I have found is that they value trust, credibility and integrity over anything else. I focus on a small network of investors who are aligned to my values and mission. These are people I enjoy spending time with and we have developed a long-term relationship. Ultimately, if you work with investors, they are placing their trust in you and your credibility is based upon your ability to deliver.

There may be other funding opportunities open to you, though. Are you aware that you can take control of your pension and choose how the money is invested? With an SASS pension investment, you can lend money to your own company, buy commercial property and lend money out to other developers for a fixed-rate return.

Speak to specialist SASS providers who can discuss this in more detail. I have mentioned it here to highlight two key areas of opportunity for you:

- Offering fixed-return investments to other landlords with SASS pensions who are looking to place their funds somewhere could open up an additional source of funding for your upcoming projects.
- You could convert your own pension into an SASS to help you fund your property portfolio growth and get a better ROI.

There may be a project you find that is too big for you, or you may decide to partner with someone else who has either the funds or the sourced deal you require. These arrangements are called joint ventures (JVs) and can be a useful way to grow with others.

I have been part of a number of successful JVs, but I would recommend you do your due diligence first as you will need to know you will still be able to work with your JV partner many years from now. What you are proposing is a business partnership, so you need to be 100% sure before you commit.

There are many types of JVs, including:

- One person provides the sourced deal, the other provides all the money
- Two people split the money and project responsibilities equally
- One person sources a large deal and passes the lead to another developer to deliver it for a small equity split
- Multiple people come together to work on a project with varying equity splits

Summary

There is a lot to think about when you're considering whether a property deal will stack or not. Do the numbers add up to deliver the ROI you want? What is the minimum ROI and cash flow you would be happy with? How much of your money are you prepared to leave in the deal? In this chapter, we have looked at these and other factors you will need to examine carefully before deciding whether to go for the deal.

We then took a look at modelling a range of schemes and exits with both planning and permitted development. When you're assessing deals in this way, it's worth taking into account your exit strategy for the future.

Finally, we examined ways of funding your project, from mortgaging to partnerships with others. It's worth remembering here that partnerships are built on trust, so don't wait until you need the money to look at this option. It's never too early to network with other property investors and build that all-important credibility.

With the deals stacking nicely, it's now time to turn our attention to stage three of the Strategy step of SPACES: where to invest.

Experienced buy to let developer Claudia had decided HMOs were the way to go; however she did not like the thought of standard HMOs. The principles of co-living resonated with her and she wanted to learn how to do it right, not just how everyone else does it. Leveraging the real life case studies and site visits, she fast tracked her knowledge of what works and what does not work, allowing her to focus her criteria and stack the best leads.

To watch the full video visit
www.theco-livingrevolution.co.uk/mastermind

FIND YOUR INVESTMENT AREA

Everybody has a different approach to sourcing an area for their property developments, but ultimately, it comes down to persistence and consistency. It is best to choose a small number of target areas so that you get to know the good from the bad. This way, you will accumulate more accurate comparable data and, over time, build up contacts who will pass you leads.

Location is one thing I have never compromised on. A good location will give you more exit options and capital appreciation over the long term.

You may pick up a cheap house in a downmarket area thinking it might appeal to a certain group of tenants. A good example of this is student accommodation on the cheaper outskirts of a city. This is fine if you *are* able to fill your HMO with students, but that tends to depend on its proximity to the university, and to amenities such as takeaway outlets, supermarkets and nightclubs. Should your influx of student tenants dry up, your cheap HMO will struggle to attract professionals. Turning it back into a family house may not be financially viable, so you may be faced with switching its use to social housing or charity leases.

The feedback I have had from housemates is that they favour central locations with good access to bus and train links. When I assess new deals, I always look at Google Maps to see how far my potential customers would need to walk to get to public transport. All of my properties are located in well-connected areas – it's all part of the excellent customer experience.

Key area information

There are some fundamentals to look for in any potential investment area. You can use a variety of online resources to gather area research data, such as Google, Wikipedia, Home, Rightmove and Zoopla. Alternatively, you can pay for software to access more in-depth information. By gathering key information on each area, you will be able to shortlist those with the most promising opportunities.

When you're assessing location, look for:

- Population size
- Median house prices

- Median rental levels
- Capital growth data
- Local employers
- Demographics and crime levels
- Transport, infrastructure and investment notes
- Highest and lowest HMO room rental rates
- Number of HMO room adverts live on SpareRoom

Shortlist target areas for co-living HMOs

Once you have done your area research, you need to centralise it all. You can do this by creating a spreadsheet with all the information you've gleaned from the bullet points in the previous section. When creating your spreadsheet, you may want to add some colour-coded notes to highlight if an area has Article 4 restrictions.

Once you have created your spreadsheet and populated all the cells with data, you then need to shortlist the front runners. Think of this as a leader board where you manually drag and drop the options into an order based on the most promising areas.

I have always used the strategy of having a small number of target areas rather than a single location. This approach ensures you are more likely to find suitable properties, even if one of the locations has little housing stock available to buy. If you operate in an Article 4 location, I suggest you look at a few nearby areas which do not have any HMO restrictions. Your ability to utilise PD will speed up your progress as you will not have to wait for planning permission.

Find the best patches for HMOs within an area

Once you have selected your target area(s), you then need to get more granular and map out the optimal patches within that location. Most towns and cities will have a number of key patches where HMOs will work best. The objective is to print out a map and draw your patch areas so that you can quickly assess any properties that become available.

If you are new to a city or town and unfamiliar with its different areas, there are a few ways you can define your patches:

- Talk to local HMO letting agents to gather their recommendations. Ask them to mark areas on a map that would be the best locations for HMOs to rent out.
- Go online and look for existing HMO maps. Some councils will provide access to HMO lists or maps. You can use this data to identify existing patches.
- Look on social media forums for landlords posting about projects in the same town or city. Scroll down their profile feeds to look for project posts, numbers and locations, adding these to your maps.

By blending all these tips together, you will start to see patterns and be able to draw a draft outline of patch areas on your own map.

Summary

The location you choose for your co-living HMO properties is vitally important. You may be able to pick up a property cheaply in an area that's out of town and maybe rather rough, but this will prove to be a false economy if you can't populate your HMO with rent-paying customers.

I tend to find customers want to be central with good access to bus and rail links. In this chapter, we have also had a look at the other things to consider when you're assessing a location, such as demographics and crime levels. With this information in hand, you can then map out the target areas for your HMOs and the patches you favour within these areas. Even if you're new to an area yourself, there are plenty of resources available to you as you do your research to find your perfect patch.

Once you have mapped out a few location options for your HMOs, it's time to decide on the types of building conversion you are going to work on.

TYPES OF BUILDING CONVERSION

I have a wide range of search criteria when it comes to the types of building conversion I intend to take on, assessing every lead based on its potential to add value or more units. The types of sites I look at include residential (flats and houses), semi commercial, full commercial, mixed use and land for new builds. In particular, I have tended to work on mixed-use commercial sites over the years as these contain a whole range of possibilities for conversion.

Let's now delve deeper into the different types of building conversion sites.

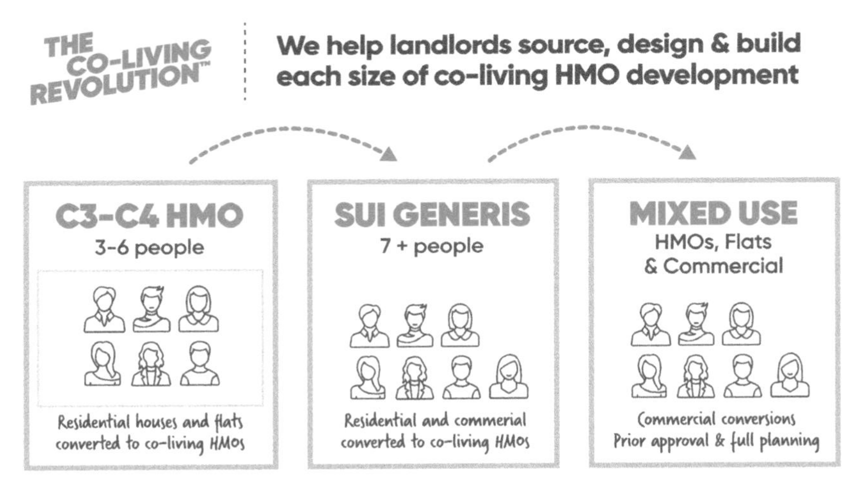

Watch some of our client case studies
Mastermind graduates share their experiences of building their own Co-Living HMOs. (www.theco-livingrevolution.co.uk)

Permitted development (PD)

I love PD! If your works fall under PD, then you don't need any planning permission (cue *loud* celebration music) if you're converting C3 residential houses into three- to six-bedroom C4 co-living HMOs, as long as you are not in an Article 4 area. This significantly reduces the complexity, risk and project timescales and can add value to your projects. Make keeping up to date with PD part of your overall co-living HMO acquisition strategy.

PD also includes side or rear extensions, roof alterations, loft conversions, porches and outbuildings. For UK developers, there is a good website called the Planning Portal that has a range of PD guides, allowing you to stay up to date with the latest changes.[15]

To complicate things a bit, there is a form of PD called prior approval. With prior approval (for example Class MA, which can enable you to turn commercial into residential apartments if you meet key criteria, or Class G that allows you to convert commercial upper floors into apartments that could be used for co-living HMOs), you need to use an architect or planning consultant to notify the local planning authority with details of the project. There are a range of prior approval types, but the main one I tend to focus on is converting commercial space into residential.

Ikea conducted a fascinating study called the 'One Shared House 2030' survey.[16] The study asked 7,000 people across 150 countries a range of questions on shared living, the answers to one of the questions identifying that respondents would like to live in tight-knit communities of four to ten people. This highlights the opportunity for you to create a mix of small C4 co-living HMOs along with medium-sized sui generis co-living HMOs.

Converting buildings in Article 4 areas

Article 4 restricts the PD rights to turn a residential C3 house into a six-bedroom C4 co-living HMO without any planning permission. You will need to wait until you have received full planning permission before starting any works and this could mean a significant period of time to cover holding costs, so your strategy for operating in Article 4 areas will need to minimise risks and delays.

In an Article 4 area, you will need to submit a full planning application to convert the building into a co-living HMO, so I would recommend you have a good planning consultant on your power team. They will be able to produce an appraisal to assess the likelihood of you achieving planning permission.

As long as the density (number of HMOs) in an area has not exceeded the Article 4 threshold, generally speaking, you should be able to get planning permission. You will, however, need to be prepared to go to appeal if the planning permission is refused.

I had a project in central Brighton that was refused planning permission, but I achieved planning on appeal. The whole process end-to-end took about eighteen months (planning application, refusal, then appeal process). I was able to operate the co-living HMO during the appeal process, giving me cash flow, but I could not remortgage and release my money until the full planning permission was granted.

Here are a few strategies to minimise risk in Article 4 areas:

- Discuss an option agreement with the seller, allowing you time to achieve planning permission
- Make an offer on buildings subject to planning
- Purchase an existing HMO in an Article 4 area with the opportunity to add further bedrooms
- Purchase buildings with fall-back schemes that are still viable if you do not achieve planning permission, such as mixed use, commercial, apartments and residential

CASE STUDY

C3 Residential Apartment to C4 Co-Living Mini-HMO

This is good example of a property that was listed on Rightmove (for everyone to see) where local knowledge really helped. I knew the apartment was in one of the top ten roads in the city and it came with full ownership of the loft. This gave me two different exit options: either a luxury three-bedroom mansion flat or a four-bedroom mini-HMO (sometimes called a mini-mo). I decided to utilise PD to convert it into a four-bedroom co-living HMO.

I offered a flexible purchase around the vendor's timescales and ensured my reconfiguration plans were approved by the free-holders prior to exchange of contracts. Although the loft was not habitable, it did feature three Velux windows, which was a bonus as I did not require any planning permission to start works. The property needed a complete re-wire, reconfiguration and loft conversion.

I relocated the kitchen to the rear of the property and knocked two rooms together to create a huge open-plan community space filled with sunlight. This space featured a high-spec kitchen, large kitchen island, lots of storage, dining space and hot desking areas. The loft room featured a private en-suite, and the remaining three rooms shared two bathrooms.

Here's a summary of the deal:

- Property sourced through Rightmove.
- Purchase price £330,000. Refurb and fit out costs approximately £75,000.
- Post-refinance mortgage 75% LTV in area of strong capital appreciation. Monthly mortgage and bills £1,831.
- Rented out as a four-bedroom co-living HMO with a monthly income of £2,910 (£34,920 annually).
- Achieved a bricks-and-mortar revaluation of £525,000.
- Total monthly profit of £1,078 (£12,936 annually) giving an ROI of 48%.
- Recycled approximately 84% of original funds after refinance.

#SOCIAL

CASE STUDY

C3 Residential House to C4 Co-Living HMO Under PD

I got a phone call one day from an estate agent about a run-down property that was about to hit the market, located right in the middle of my target town with no Article 4 restrictions. As I only lived a short distance away, I dropped everything and was there within the hour, ensuring that I was the first through the door.

Because I had been clear on my criteria, the agent knew only to call me about larger than average properties that could become HMOs. This particular building already had over 25 sqm of kitchen and social space at the rear and an original loft, so I knew straight away I could easily get six rooms out of it under PD. The location was perfect for professionals or students as it was in the middle of the town.

Given the condition of the property, the vendor was looking for certainty of sale and was happy to work with a local developer who could buy the property quickly. We managed to negotiate a small discount on the price and avoided an open market bidding war. Before we had even exchanged contracts, I had already drawn up the architectural plan, designed the layout and created a tendering pack.

The property was across three floors with a strange loft that did not meet building regulations due to the entrance access and lack of insulation. However, the room sizes were big and offered a lot of scope for reconfiguration. Unlike other houses in the road, this one came with a rear extension, but unfortunately it was single-skin brickwork which would require updating to meet current building regulations. The property featured a good-sized garden with plenty of scope to redesign and turn it into a community space.

For the refurbishment, I worked with a local builder sourced via a tendering process. I reconfigured the house to provide six good-sized bedrooms, five bathrooms and an additional toilet. A loft and rear extension upgrade meant they met building regulations, and I installed a full unvented heating system to ensure decent showers for all housemates.

For the co-living HMO end product, I created design-led bedrooms with plenty of storage, comfort and project stations so my customers could work from home. The community space consisted of a large café kitchen with plenty of storage and seating for all, space to hot desk, a dedicated mini cinema room/breakout space, and a large landscaped garden with dining area, outdoor chill-out seating, private relaxation nook, barbecue zone and bike store.

Here's a summary of the deal:

- Property sourced through a local estate agent.
- Purchase price £330,000. Refurb and fit out costs approximately £115,000.
- Post-refinance mortgage 80% LTV in area of strong capital appreciation. Monthly mortgage and bills £2,331.
- Rented out as a six-bedroom co-living HMO with a monthly income of £4,170 (£50,040 annually).
- Achieved a bricks-and-mortar revaluation of £525,000.
- Total monthly profit of £1,838 (£22,056 annually) giving an ROI of 47%.
- Recycled approximately 75% of original funds after refinance.

Commercial/residential into sui generis HMOs

If you are planning to create a co-living space with seven or more bedrooms, then you need to submit a full planning application for a sui generis HMO. There are many ways you can develop a building into a sui generis HMO, but I would always recommend having a good local planning consultant as part of your power team so that you can complete a planning appraisal prior to any application.

For many of the properties I purchase, I design multiple schemes as fall-back plans in case I don't achieve sui generis planning permission. As long as the fall-back plans stack up as a deal, I am happy to take the risk to buy unconditionally.

Here are a few examples of buildings you can convert into sui generis HMOs:

- A large private house
- A commercial building
- Part of a building/scheme
- An existing HMO

One of the key appeals of a sui generis HMO is the additional cash flow from a large number of rentable rooms.

As part of your planning application, you will need to refer to national planning standards rather than local HMO licensing standards. As an example, room sizes are slightly larger for national planning compared with local licensing. A good architect and planning consultant can work with you to check that your potential plans meet the planning standards criteria.

CASE STUDY

Commercial Building Into Sui Generis Co-Living HMO

This lead was a retail shop on the ground floor with residential accommodation above, owned by a company that had left the building vacant. The building was 182 sqm across three floors with scope to extend further at the rear. It was centrally located in the town with great transport links and amenities nearby.

Although the property was on the open market, most investors were put off by a title restriction preventing conversion to HMOs or flats. I decided to approach the company behind this and successfully agreed a price to lift all restrictions.

I designed two schemes with this site. The first scheme was to convert the ground floor into two apartments via prior approval and reconfigure the upper floors to a co-living HMO under PD.

The second scheme combined the whole building, requiring full planning permission to create an eight-bedroom sui generis co-living HMO with the addition of a rear extension. After receiving planning permission for both schemes, I decided to build out scheme two as it had a higher GDV and cash flow.

The refurbishment was managed using the schedule of works (SOW) templates and tendering process we'll discuss in Chapter 11. In addition to the rear extension, the building required extensive insulation upgrades and a new unvented heating system. All bedrooms were a decent size, ranging from 10–20 sqm with plenty of storage, seating areas and projects stations to work from home. The social space I created was over 25 sqm and featured a central island table for all housemates to socialise. Several rooms featured private outside patios and there was a dedicated bike store for all housemates.

Here's a summary of the deal:

- Property sourced through a local letting agent.
- Purchase price £240,000 (including lifting restriction). Refurb and fit out costs approximately £170,000.
- Post-refinance mortgage 75% LTV. Monthly mortgage and bills £2,620.
- Rented out as an eight-bedroom co-living HMO with a monthly income of £4,800 (£57,600 annual).
- Achieved an investment revaluation of £650,000.
- Total monthly profit of £2,201 (£26,419 annually), giving an ROI of 657%.
- Recycled approximately 99% of original funds after refinance.

Commercial into residential and mixed use

Over the years, I have worked on a number of commercial to mixed-use residential projects. This means that within the development, there are a range of planning classes that could include co-living HMOs, apartments, office and retail.

These projects offer a great way to revitalise the dated high-street model with planning changes such as Class MA and Class G. Given that professionals and students love to live in central locations, this provides a huge opportunity for your future developments. In mixed-use developments, I reduce down the retail spaces with flexible lease terms. This provides low-cost retail space or offices to small businesses and local entrepreneurs.

A key benefit of mixed use is a blend of revenue streams. For example, you will have money coming in from a co-living HMO rented by the room, longer-term rents from apartments and even longer leases from commercial tenants. Although single lets (apartments) don't get as much attention as co-living HMOs due to their lower income, it's important to remember tenants will tend to stay in apartments longer and pay all the bills. I always recommend building a diverse portfolio blending high-yielding co-living HMOs with lower-yielding apartments and commercial spaces.

CASE STUDY

Commercial Building Into Mixed Use

I heard about this site via a local commercial agent. It was on the open market, but was in a run-down condition and required extensive works, so many investors were put off. Location-wise, it was on a secondary high street with great transport links.

The property was a derelict convenience store with a huge ancillary rear extension for storage. The upper floors were residential, but could only be accessed via the shop. All the roofs required urgent repairs and a secondary rear extension was in a bad way.

Under prior approval, I achieved planning permission to convert the rear of the commercial space into further residential units, retaining a small retail unit to the high-street frontage. I repaired the main roof and replaced all the flat roofs across the building. The secondary rear extension needed completely re-building as it was not structurally sound, but the huge single storey rear extension was well built and only needed to be brought up to building regulations standards.

I converted the upper floors under PD into a five-bedroom co-living HMO with social space and additional breakout space. The rear extension was converted into a two-bedroom apartment with outdoor space which I rented out by the room under the same co-living HMO product. I leased the small retail unit to a barber who signed a five-year full repairing lease (which means the tenant is responsible for all repairs, upkeep and buildings insurance on the property).

Here's a summary of the deal:

- Property sourced through a local estate agent.
- Purchase price £190,000. Refurb and fit out costs approximately £225,000.
- Post-refinance mortgage 75% LTV. Monthly mortgage and bills £3,145.
- Rented out as a five-bedroom co-living HMO plus a two-bedroom co-living apartment plus a small retail unit with a monthly income of £4,650 (£55,800 annually).
- Achieved an investment revaluation of £650,000.
- Total monthly profit of £1,505 (£18,060 annual) giving an ROI of infinite.[17]
- Recycled over 100% of original funds after refinance.

CASSETTELORD

Build to rent

If you are feeling ambitious and want to build from the ground up, then build to rent is a fast-growing trend in the UK. Build to rent describes apartment blocks that have been built exclusively for renters and are owned and managed by a single landlord.

Your entire sourcing strategy will need to change for this one as you move into land acquisition. Good examples of build to rent are Fizzy Living[18] and Moda Living.[19] These are projects with hundreds of rooms on a huge scale. Build to rent projects are hybrids of co-living, apartments, co-working, offices, gyms and retail.

Of course, you may not want to create hundreds of rooms in a tower block and take on that level of risk, but build to rent still offers you an opportunity to develop lower-risk small- to medium-sized schemes in line with customer research. By exploring a hybrid of co-living HMOs, co-working and apartments, you can provide a customer lifecycle that stretches beyond the rented bedroom model.

Summary

When it comes to deciding on the type of development you wish to take on, there are different options to consider, including PD, converting buildings in Article 4 areas, sui generis HMOs, converting commercial properties into residential and mixed-use spaces, and build to rent. PD is a great option, especially if you're just starting out as you don't need to wait for planning permission and risk it being refused, but the more risk you take as you gain experience, the better the ROI.

We now come to the final stage of the Strategy step of SPACES. It's time to look at how to source your property-development deals.

Find out how experienced developer Neelam decided to upskill her knowledge of co-living HMOs to create a high-quality product in line with her values. Using techniques and detailed case studies shared on The Co-Living Mastermind™, Neelam has filled her pipeline with off-market commercial to residential leads. She now actively targets properties on the high street where others have missed the potential.

To watch the full video visit
www.theco-livingrevolution.co.uk/mastermind

TECHNIQUES FOR SOURCING DEALS

The strategy step of your SPACES model is almost complete. All that you need to do now is source the deals for property developments that will lead you towards financial freedom. If you follow the guidelines in this chapter, you will add the right sourcing methods and techniques into your strategy and you won't go far wrong.

The art of finding and stacking properties is one of the most important skills you can have as a developer. If you have any blockers on area research, deal analysis or building types, then you need to deal with these urgently before frustration sets in. Once you are happy with these, then it is time to go hunting for deals!

Online platforms

Even though estate agents may call you about new leads, online listing portals are a great way to ensure you do not miss anything that may have slipped through the net. Unless you are calling agents regularly, these portals are a far better way to review all the new properties appearing on the market.

Once you have identified your patches within your investment areas, you can then set up notifications on listing portals to email you when any new sites meeting your criteria appear in your patches. Most listing portals will allow you to draw patches on a map and save them as part of your criteria for notifications.

I would recommend starting with online platforms such as Rightmove, Zoopla, PrimeLocation, Rightmove Commercial and EGI Propertylink. It is also worth making a note of all the key residential and commercial agents in your target areas, as sometimes properties appear on their websites before they make their way to the listing portals.

Working with estate agents

Estate agents can provide a healthy flow of new leads for you. If you purchase quickly and without any issues, this will build your credibility with agents and they will be more likely to call you before other investors. The key strategy with agents is to make sure that you always get the call first.

Visit your local estate agents and let them know of your plans and what you are looking for. Get your first site secured (to prove credibility), and then take the agent for a coffee to discuss your wider plans for more sites. You need to build relationships and nurture them over time, so don't forget to follow up with agents regularly to make sure you are top of their lists when new leads arrive.

A simple way to do this is to add reminders to your calendar. Alternatively, if you are happy using technology, a customer relationship management system with auto reminders will do the job for you.

Direct to vendor (off market)

This technique, of course, relies on the owner wanting to sell. It is a manual way of doing things, but it does work as when you enter into a direct one-to-one conversation with the owner, you are not bidding against other developers. Once you know your target area, you will be able to laser focus on a set of roads and identify any properties there that fit your criteria.

There are a number of ways you can use the direct-to-vendor method:

- Targeted leaflet dropping in key areas
- Sending letters to landlords via the publicly available HMO register
- Walking the streets looking for run-down properties and opportunities
- If you're in the UK, using the Land Registry on the GOV website to find out who owns a property
- Using property land software to identify sites that meet your criteria

Technology can help you locate new leads that are not on the market yet and target their owners. Software can access Ordnance Survey maps, planning history, use classes and owner details at a click of a button. When you combine this information with Google Earth, you have a powerful suite of tools to locate and assess possible sites for co-living HMOs in minutes. During our mastermind deal clinics we often use them live to assess potential sites.

Property sourcers

Property sourcers can identify sites that you may have missed, even with all the techniques we have already covered. Most property sourcers will charge a fee for finding and packaging a property deal, so you could even turn the tables and take on property sourcing yourself as a way to raise funds to buy your first assets.

When you're looking to work with a property sourcer, always do your due diligence. Google the backgrounds of the sourcers to make sure they are credible. Even though property sourcers package deals, they may be optimistic on key numbers within their spreadsheets. I would recommend you stress test every deal yourself and create a deal-stacking sheet. The property sourcer's objective is to sell you a deal for a fee; your objective is to ensure that it is in fact a good deal and the numbers are accurate.

Networking

Networking is a great way both to find new sites and to pass on leads that are not suitable for you to others. Being visible and active at events and on social media will increase your chances of becoming trusted in the property-development community. Many landlords have leads that they are not planning on progressing themselves and want to hand on to someone else, so network to make sure you're the one they call.

There are many physical property events; however one I would recommend is Property Investors Network (pin). Every month pin hosts networking events in most major cities around the UK where you can listen to some inspiring talks and meet other local property investors.

If you have never been to a pin event before, you can attend free of charge as my guest by using the voucher code 'Sscott'. All of the monthly networking events are listed on www.pinmeeting.co.uk. Your professional network is also a great source of leads. For example, your architects may be aware of new sites in the process of obtaining planning permission. Your letting agent may be aware of landlords deciding to sell off properties they bought many years ago that have scope to be modernised or reconfigured.

Risks, challenges and issues

Unfortunately, in property developing, there are lots of things that can go wrong along the way, so your strategy needs to prepare you for an emotional rollercoaster. It would be amazing if everything went according to plan, but things will come up and you need a strategy to deal with them.

Here are just a few challenges I have had along the way:

- A JV partnership that turned bad. The person we partnered with did not have the experience they'd claimed to have, and it cost myself and my business partner a lot of time and money to get them out of the company.
- Issues with defective building work that were not picked up on survey as they were hidden. We have had to rebuild foundations, piers, steels and extensions at significant cost and time delay.
- A builder asked for our help temporarily housing one of his tradespeople. After this person moved into one of our co-living HMOs, we had lots of anti-social issues from them, leading to many tenants leaving the property and costly legal action.
- We've had to pull out of projects when surveys have thrown up heavy remedial and structural work that would have made the projects unviable. With vendors unwilling to budge, fall-back schemes become less viable and only the best outcome may stack.
- It can be challenging and costly managing variations when builders add extras without sign off and clear understanding of the sign off process.

The list is endless. These things will happen and it will get stressful at times, but a lot of the models and processes I use today have been built from learning from my mistakes. You will need perseverance to achieve your goals, and resilience and focus to deal with challenges. Build a support network of trusted advisers around you and they will help you minimise risk along the way.

Summary

In this chapter, we have looked at a range of deal sourcing techniques so that you can spot more potential properties when searching for sites. The resources for finding your next great deal include online portals, estate agents, going direct to the vendor, using property sourcers and networking. Finally, we had a look at some of the risks involved in property developments of any size. Armed with this knowledge, you can design a strategy that not only helps you build a fantastic property portfolio and the financial freedom that brings, but also mitigates the risks.

Having a solid strategy will help you hit your goals. To achieve results, you need to remove blockers and have a clear vision of where you are heading. It would be easy to skip this strategy section and get stuck in, but later down the line, you would find you're spending much of your time looking at the wrong properties in the wrong areas and missing opportunities. This part has been about setting you up for results, giving you focus and putting the correct strategy in place.

Now you have your property strategy covered, it's time to move on to Part Three which is all about creating the best co-living HMO product on the market. Let's jump on in!

Bonus Content

Visit **www.theco-livingrevolution.co.uk/bonus**
for your free content, checklists and resources to help you get started on your co-living HMO journey.

PART THREE _
PRODUCT

INNOVATION PROCESS

As landlords and developers, we need to design and build products that are valuable and enjoyable for the end user. Our tenants are our customers and our properties are our product line. As with any good product, we need to adapt and evolve our offering continually to stay ahead of the curve.

If you are developing a product to sell or rent to a customer, then you need to compete on the market. Product innovation is about identifying customer problems and imagining new solutions that improve the customer experience. This encompasses many areas, such as customer research, design, prototyping, building and testing.

Innovation is not some secret that only a few know; it is a step-by-step process that anyone can learn. Allow me to introduce you to the Co-Living HMO Innovation Canvas that my company uses on our Co-Living Mastermind programme. This canvas is based on the same design thinking processes I fine-tuned over twenty-five years of running product innovation teams. It can help you design and build the best co-living HMOs in your area and stay one step ahead of the competition.

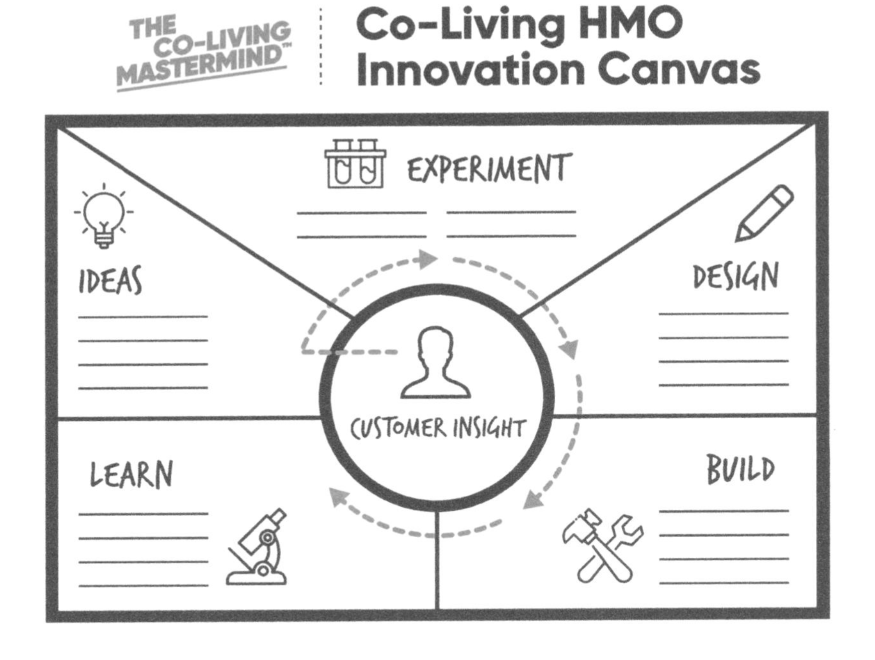

PRODUCTS
NEED TO
CONSTANTLY
EVOLVE TO
SURVIVE.

THE
CO-LIVING
REVOLUTION™

The Co-Living HMO Innovation Canvas is split into six stages: customer insight, ideas, experiment, design, build and learn. Together, all the stages work in a constant loop which will ensure your product is always adapting and evolving. This is the reason many of my co-living concepts are several years in advance of HMO trends. You too can use this simple system to build co-living HMOs that genuinely improve people's lives and achieve your financial goals.

In this chapter, we will look at the first three stages of the canvas.

Customer insight

The playing field has changed. No longer can you push outdated HMOs and expect to fill them with tenants. The customer has moved on and so have your competitors; co-living represents a seismic shift towards customer-focused design.

Never before has it been so important to understand your customer. The customer chooses where to spend their money, so you need to be their first and only choice.

I have used a whole range of user-research techniques over the years, but my favourite approach is known as gorilla research. This method is about faster, cheaper and less formal ways to gather customer insight to make business decisions.

Two key gorilla techniques I recommend you start with are face-to-face interviews (in person or over Zoom) and email-based surveys. If you are an existing landlord, you will already have a customer list to contact. Email surveys of seven to ten questions increase your volume of measurable data and can be sent to your customers to be completed when it is convenient for them. Face-to-face interviews are a great way to find out more in-depth information beyond email surveys and allow you to ask additional questions to understand why an answer was given.

A customer survey I conducted with my company many years ago showed that some of my tenants worked from home a few days per week. I was then able to use this knowledge to prototype a new 'live/work' concept where we added co-working spaces into co-living HMOs.

When Covid came along, suddenly far more people were working from home, but we were among the few landlords already providing the facilities they needed.

Ongoing customer research like this will feed into your ideas phase, allowing you to constantly evolve your product.

Ideas

Fresh ideas are the lifeblood of any business. They can propel you to the top of the market and add rocket fuel to your growth. I call the process of creating new ideas 'ideation', but others refer to it as 'brainstorming'. Either way, it is one of the most exciting stages of the innovation canvas as its aim is to come up with large quantities of new ideas that can be filtered down to the best ones.

There is a common misconception that only creative people can come up with ideas. This has not been my experience in the business world. Over the years, I have run thousands of ideas workshops and actively encouraged input from a broad spectrum of attendees, many of whom would not consider themselves creative. This diverse input is what generates angles and avenues that may not have been considered before.

What many people lack is creative confidence, as described in the book of the same name by Tom and David Kelley.[20] Good design thinking is about tapping into the broad knowledge pool and encouraging people, whatever their background, to contribute their perspectives. Even if you're building your portfolio as an individual, there are still plenty of people you can ask to contribute to your ideation, such as your property developers' network, family and friends, or your current tenants if you already have some. Ideation is one of the most important factors in enabling successful companies to innovate.

For your own creativity, you need to increase the number of inputs and your visual stimulation. This will give your mind a rich source of information to synthesise. Inspiration is all around you every day, and subconsciously, your mind is absorbing everything. I read lots of design books, non-fiction books, look on social media and constantly photograph the physical world to stimulate my creativity.

Look to increase the amount of visual information you absorb. Build a mood board with pictures of things that inspire you. Look to unrelated markets (like hotels or your favourite clothing brands) for inspiration. Ideas may not fully form in the first ideation session, sometimes you need to step away for a few days and allow your sub conscious mind time to connect the dots. Before you know it, you mind will likely be filled with inspiration and an excitement to get started.

Creativity can be nurtured just like anything else through building confidence, ongoing support and following proven design processes (we'll get on to 'Design' in the next two chapters). One of the reasons I created this book and started mentoring landlords was to provide a model that could help anyone regardless of their backgrounds create a better product and customer experience. You can spend your life chasing design trends, but if you do, you will always be reliant on getting ideas from others. I want this section to show you that you can harnesses creativity and generate your own rich pool of new ideas.

Experiment

Think of your first co-living HMO project as one big experiment containing lots of prototypes. As you gather valuable feedback, you can then refine your next co-living HMO. It is this constant iteration that drives your product and the customer experience forward. The beauty of this approach is that it is led by customer insight.

Prototyping is a powerful tool as it allows you to experiment with new ideas, engage with your customer and constantly evolve your product. If you take a mobile phone or a car as an example, each new model is different to the last. This evolution of the product is driven by the designers testing prototypes, gathering user feedback and simplifying the usability. Your co-living space is your product. You would never create a product without updating it.

Try to incorporate experimental prototypes every year to test new ideas. These prototypes can be anything from a custom headboard or a layout concept to a new piece of software – anything that will improve customer experience. Think about what prototypes you could test in your own co-living HMOs.

Summary

In this chapter, we have covered the first three stages of the Co-Living HMO Innovation Canvas. Customer insight, new ideas and experimenting ensure you are always evolving your product in line with customer needs. All products have to evolve or risk becoming obsolete as customers go elsewhere, so these three stages lay the foundations for the more involved design stage of the canvas.

We will look at design in detail over the next two chapters, 'Space Design Concepts' and 'The Space Design Blueprint'. This is not to say the design stage of the canvas is more important than the others, just that it takes more time and expertise to get it right. Finally, we will round this 'Product' part of the book off with a look at 'Build And Learn', covering working with tradespeople to successfully deliver your co-living HMO product, and how to learn, adapt and improve your product.

Examples of a feature wall and headboard prototype we experimented with

SPACE DESIGN CONCEPTS

When you're designing a new co-living HMO, the first thing you need to do is refer to the research you did in the customer insight stage of the Co-Living HMO Innovation Canvas. It is this rich data that feeds into the space design approach.

I like to use the term 'space design' as it encompasses architectural, environmental and interior design. Interior design will often deal with the space as it is, while at the architectural stage, you have a unique opportunity to alter the layout and composition of the building structurally. The challenging thing here is that architects are not likely to be involved in all the other stages of the innovation canvas, so their solution will only be based on their limited knowledge of co-living HMOs.

This is where you come in. You don't need to know about the structural elements as that is the architect's job; what you need to focus on is the space from the customer's perspective. By transforming spaces through considered design, you can create amazing living environments. Design influences the structure, layout, interior and exterior of the HMO, so the biggest wins in the design process come before any interior work has even started.

Architectural and layout design

The largest opportunity in any co-living HMO development is when a building is modified and adapted at the architectural level. Simple changes can increase volume, open-plan a space, modify flow and provide further bedrooms. This creative use of design can transform your project and have a huge impact on ROI and the customer experience.

At this stage, I recommend you work in close collaboration with an architect to design many iterations of layouts. A combination of their structural building experience and your customer perspective will allow you to design better spaces. One of the first things to do in any project is to get the building measured up so that you can work on alternative schemes. I often book in the measure up as soon as I have secured the project off the market, so that I can start designing during the conveyancing period. Once you have a rough outline of a design, you can then add more detail such as café kitchens, social spaces and bedrooms.

By incorporating open-plan spaces into your design, you can create an engaging and inspiring central community space. In addition to these open-plan spaces, smaller breakout spaces in non-habitable sized rooms and large hallways give the customers somewhere to get away from the buzz of communal living if they wish. Working with a good architect is the cornerstone of your ability to create desirable co-living HMOs.

Social vs privacy

When you're designing co-living HMOs with your architect, always be mindful to balance social and private spaces. While it's likely to be true that the customer is looking to improve their social lifestyle, they may also have concerns about lack of privacy when joining a co-living community. The Ikea 'One Shared House 2030' survey found that the respondents' biggest concern about living in an HMO is a lack of privacy.[21] If you can address this problem, then your co-living HMO will be more appealing to customers.

The spaces that you create will fall into three categories. They will be either large social, semi social or private. You may find that some multi-use spaces fall within two categories based on how the customer interacts with them.

Large social spaces are high-traffic areas and the focal point of the community. Every part of their design is about bringing people together and creating opportunities for socialising. These large social spaces can include café kitchens, cinema rooms, co-working spaces, barbecue zones and landscaped outdoor areas.

Semi-social spaces are slightly lower-traffic areas where customers can both socialise and relax. Many multi-use spaces find themselves in this category, for example breakout spaces, small cinema spaces, outdoor seating zones and co-working spaces.

The balance of social vs privacy

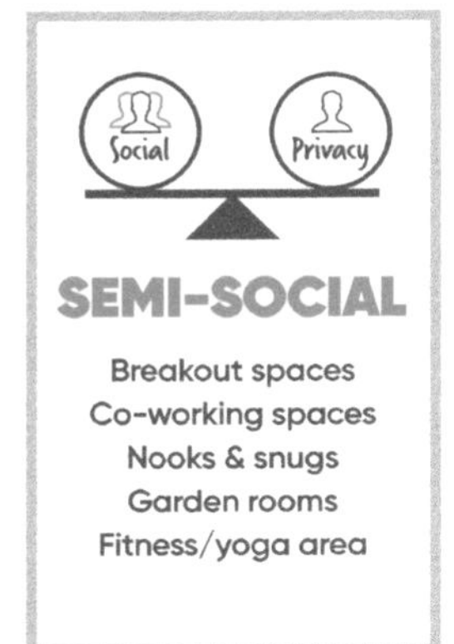

Private spaces are all about relaxation and a comfortable, secluded place away from the busy community. Sometimes, we all need a bit of quiet time to ourselves. Being aware of this, you can design a balance of spaces leading to a better living experience for the customer and longer-term occupancy. Along with comfortable bedrooms, areas such as breakout spaces and private nooks provide an opportunity for your customer to gain privacy when they need it.

Designing for flow

When you're creating your co-living HMO, an important consideration is the flow of people through the spaces, as you are often dealing with a large number of people sharing amenities. By analysing how people use an environment, you can optimise layouts and place furniture in the most suitable locations. Understanding the flow through the spaces in your co-living HMO will also reveal high- and low-visited areas and give you a glimpse into customer behaviour.

In high-traffic areas such as social spaces, plan out possible walking routes through the space to identify any pinch points and explore alternate layouts. When you're working with fairly small spaces, it is vitally important to consider carefully how layout options will affect flow and use.

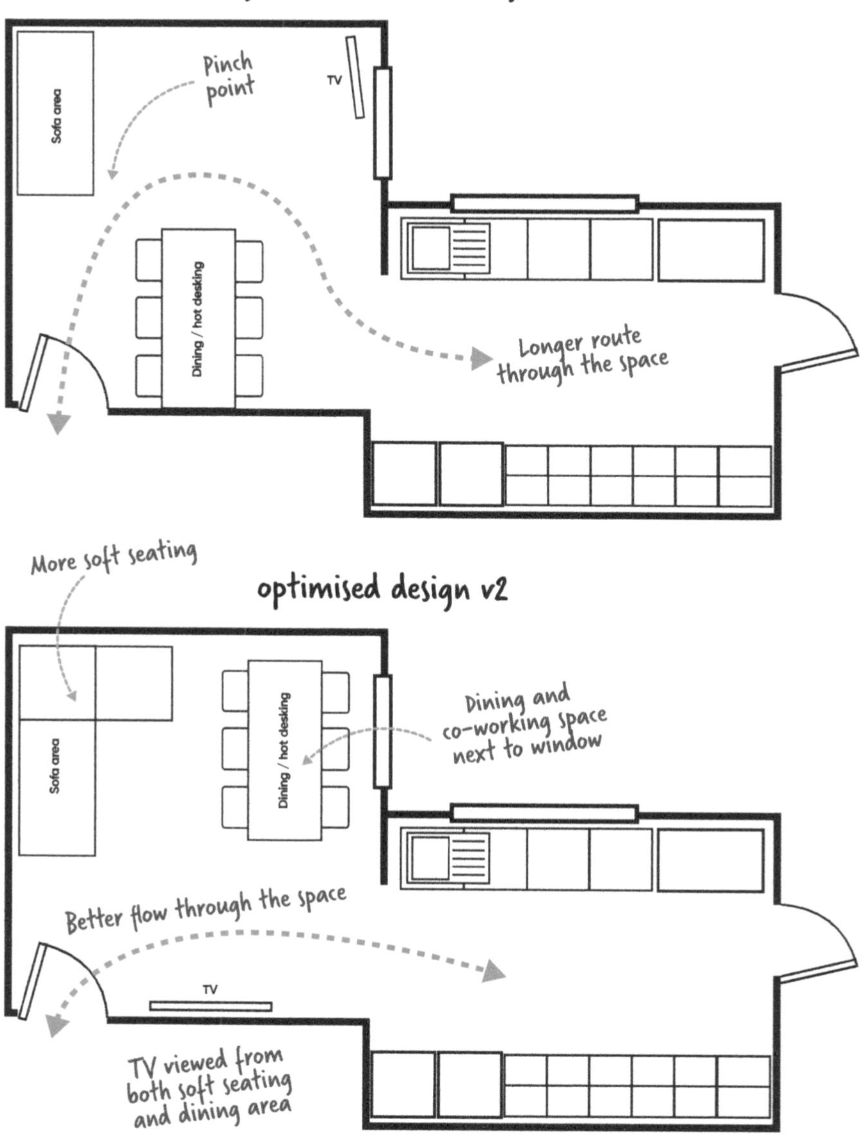

This floor plan shows how moving the table layout achieved a more useable space with a natural flow through the rooms.

Adaptive multi-use space

Customers are looking for spaces that are flexible and adaptable to accommodate their needs. We can see the basic principles of multi-use space all around us, from events venues transformed into fitness spaces to cafés transformed into night-time wine bars. This adaptability in the commercial world leads to increased revenue and higher footfall. With more people moving to urban living, multi-use space design in a co-living HMO can help make buildings more sustainable for the future.

A good example of a multi-use space is a co-working hub. During the day, these spaces, which have large workshop tables, private work pods and large-scale monitors, are used for work. During breakfast, lunch and dinner times, these same spaces provide overflow dining with large tables and monitors that become TVs. If you just add private work pods, then this space has no scope to be converted into a dining room. Good design enables the customer to get more convenience from less space.

Example of a co-working space that can be used for overflow dining and meetings outside of working time.

PAGES
LIVING

Biophilic design and wellbeing

Biophilic means love of nature, so biophilic design is about bringing nature closer to people and improving their connection to the natural environment. Over the years, cities have separated us from nature. With more people living in urban centres, there has been a rise in mental health issues and loneliness. We need to redress the balance. The biophilic design movement is about redesigning spaces to become healthy habitats in an ever-changing world, improving wellbeing, reducing stress and boosting both creativity and productivity.

Here are a few tips for you to incorporate biophilic design into your projects:

- Use plants within the physical space
- Use artificial elements of nature, eg artificial plants and green walls
- Increase natural light and improve views of nature
- Use recycled natural materials and natural colours
- Include recuperative breakout spaces and nooks containing plants

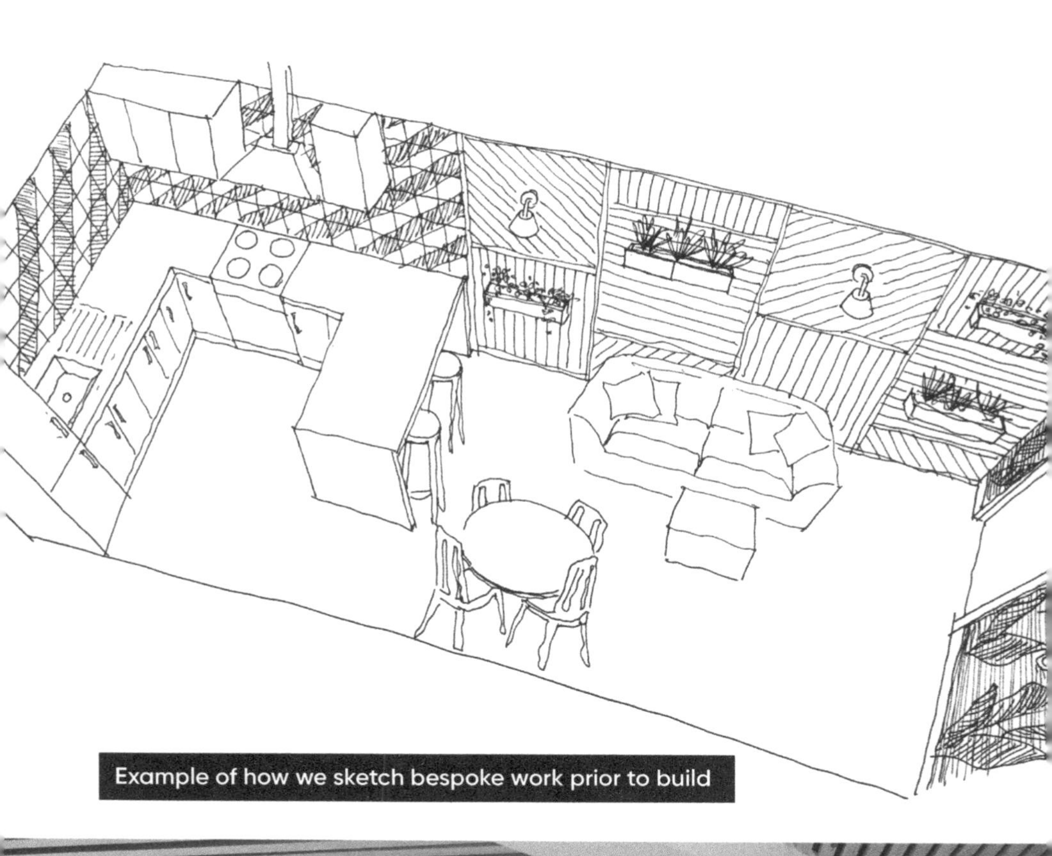

Example of how we sketch bespoke work prior to build

Bespoke design

Have you ever noticed that a lot of HMOs look the same? That is because many HMO training courses recommend the same approach and suppliers for fit out. This is something my company Co-Living Spaces does *not* do. If you are looking to create the most desirable product on the market, the chances are you will need to step away from off-the-shelf solutions like HMO furniture packs and embrace a more bespoke approach.

Approach social spaces in your co-living HMO as key community areas, focusing on bespoke fit-outs designed for social interaction. Working with a carpenter and electrician, you can take ideas from simple sketches through to build. Many items that are difficult to source, such as private work pods, seating areas, bespoke lighting, feature walls and custom headboards, can be created by your carpenter and electrician.

Through the use of bespoke work, you can bring your ideas to life. Work closely with your builders and use a 'design appendix', which we discuss in Chapter 11, to launch new product ideas.

Simplicity and usability

There are many principles that inform good design, but one of the most consistent is simplicity. Time and time again, designers rush to add functions and controls to their product which only serve to confuse the customer. Only when you consider things from the customer's perspective can you strip away the unnecessary and focus on the essential.

In many ways, it can be harder to take things away than it is to add them, but the customer generally does not want complexity. They will be attracted to well-designed products that display simplicity and ease of use.

When you're designing co-living HMOs, focus on designing for purpose. You are not recreating the family house; you are purposely designing a space for a group of people to share. In doing so, you need to deliver spaces that are simple to use and foster interaction and community.

Keeping things simple does not mean your design style needs to be plain. Simplicity is all about how easy something is to use and how it makes your customers feel. Every brand needs a personality and a brand style, which we will cover in Chapter 12, so there is scope to be brave and experimental with the finishing layer of your co-living HMO product. There is no point having great usability if the product is bland and does not appeal to the customer. You are selling an experience, which means finding the perfect blend of brand style and usability.

It's no surprise to learn that easy-to-use products are more successful than complex ones. If your co-living HMO is well designed, your customer will enjoy using the space without getting frustrated, so consider this at the design stage.

Look at things from a human perspective. Have you provided enough different types of storage? To answer this, you need to understand what items your customers will bring with them and how they store them in the rooms. How about lighting? Do they have options to set different light levels? What about the bed? Is it comfortable? Are the materials you have used durable?

The list is endless. Work your way around your co-living HMO room by room and think about usability as part of your design process. To achieve great usability, you need to think like the customer. Usability affects customer satisfaction, which in turn affects your occupancy, so it is an important consideration.

Summary

In this chapter, we have discussed a range of design concepts to help you create better spaces, including how architectural design can provide the biggest wins, getting the correct balance of social vs private spaces, considering the flow of people through a space, getting more from less with multi-use space, improving wellbeing with biophilic design, creating a unique product with bespoke work and ensuring good usability through simplicity.

Taking a design-led approach will ensure your products always:

- Attract more enquiries
- Achieve higher room rents
- Maximise the property's end value
- Drive longer-term occupancy

Unlike traditional HMOs, co-living offers the customer a range of facilities to enhance their experience and foster a community, so you need to place an emphasis on creating awesome social spaces to help bring housemates together. Café kitchens, cinema rooms, co-working and breakout spaces, games and fitness rooms, private nooks, roof terraces, barbecue zones and landscaped outdoor spaces can directly affect the way people feel. Using biophilic design, you can blur the line between indoor and outdoor spaces and improve customer wellbeing.

By taking a customer-centred approach, you will design spaces that drive higher occupancy.

SPACE DESIGN BLUEPRINT

Would you like to have the most in-demand co-living HMOs in your area that achieve the highest rents?

In this chapter, I will show you how you can use the Space Design Blueprint during your design phase to create a range of co-living HMO facilities and spaces. We will be covering social spaces, co-working, bedroom and other private spaces, along with technology and support.

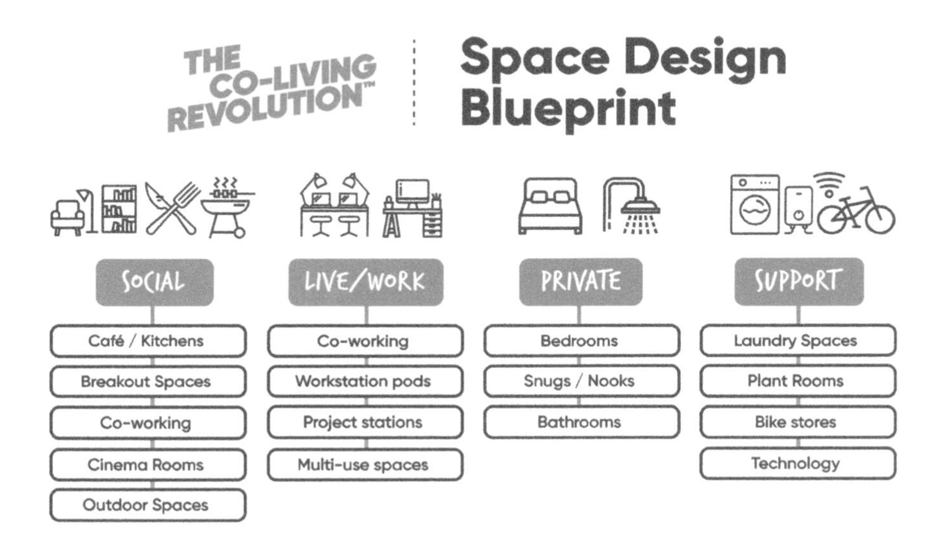

Create amazing social spaces

One of the three pillars of co-living is community. If you are looking to build a thriving co-living HMO community, it's important to have a good range of well-designed spaces that encourage people to eat, socialise, collaborate, live, work and play together.

The key word here is 'together'. When you're working at the architectural and design level, it's essential to keep this in mind as it can have a huge impact on the layout of your co-living HMOs.

Café kitchens

Let's start with the obvious co-living space: the kitchen and dining area. What is the most important element that can help build a community in this space? If you have a six-bedroom co-living property and the only eating area is a breakfast bar with two stools and a sofa opposite a TV, would this create a community? If your only dining space is a high table with stools facing a wall, would that build a community? No, it's not Costa Coffee!

If housemates are unable to eat and socialise together, then it's just another HMO with a fancy name. You want the housemates to interact with one another. The kitchen is the central hub of the community, so you need to design it to accommodate large groups and multiple people cooking at the same time. When you're designing co-living kitchens, it's important to focus on providing enough eating space for the community to sit together. It is at mealtimes when social bonds and friendships are formed.

One of the first concepts my company Co-Living Spaces launched many years ago was the café kitchen. Inspired interiors, multiple seating zones and a casual café feel re-imagined this space into an environment housemates would enjoy spending time in, just like their favourite café.

This semi-commercial approach focuses on the usability of the kitchen and optimising the layout for multiple uses throughout the day. Unfortunately, though, it's likely that your architect will not be a kitchen designer and your kitchen designer will not understand HMOs. It's down to you to feedback to them what you need to achieve with the space.

I recommend getting suitable online floorplan software and doing it yourself. Ask your architect to send you the plans with key dimensions. This way, you can recreate them to design the layout, storage and functionality of the space. When working on layout, you will need to balance the needs of kitchen functionality and eating areas.

Look to blend a mix of formal and casual seating areas in café kitchens that range from large benches and tables to more comfortable soft seating. It is good to give the housemates a range of options on how to use the space, but remember, it is important to have a main dining area that can accommodate all housemates for group meals should they decide to eat together.

Examples of our co-living HMO café kitchens

afe
Co
Co-Hub
Space.
CASSETTELORD

Breakout spaces and private nooks

As much as we crave social interaction, we humans sometimes require a more peaceful area. When you're designing co-living HMOs, you need to find a balance between social and private areas that works for the customer.

A breakout space is any secluded area away from the main social space with comfortable seating and no distractions. Customers can go to these spaces to retreat from their busy lives. A breakout space can have a variety of uses in a co-living HMO: a workspace to boost creativity, collaborate in small groups or work alone on a personal project; a private space to catch up with a visiting friend; or an oasis of calm where housemates can switch off and relax, helping to promote good mental health. The term 'breakout space' originates from office and tech startups to describe spaces for employees to gather into small groups to have ad-hoc meetings, brainstorm ideas or take a break.

Another name for a small breakout space is a nook. A nook is a secluded spot which is separate from the rest of the room. An example of a nook is a quiet place for reading or studying.

The great thing about a breakout space or nook is that the customer can choose how to use it, and so they define what it is. Breakout spaces should be comfortable, thoughtfully designed areas where people enjoy spending their time. Having these additional peaceful spaces encourages more movement around the building and promotes health and wellbeing.

Breakout spaces are a great way to address the balance between socialising and privacy within a co-living community.

Outdoor spaces

Outdoor spaces are often overlooked by landlords and developers, but they are a prime opportunity to extend the co-living HMO experience. When designed well, these spaces can encourage customers to socialise, eat together and relax together even more. We all tend to spend a vast amount of our time indoors, so access to outdoor spaces and nature will improve housemates' mental health and wellbeing.

To make sure your customers enjoy the outside space, provide suitable seating areas and consider the location of the sun. Seating can be either bespoke or purchased, but as with the interior spaces, it is important to provide enough for the whole community. Make sure the plants you choose are low maintenance and durable as you or your handy man will have to visit the site regularly to maintain the communal areas.

Outdoor spaces should be fun, inspiring environments that people look forward to spending time in, so dedicate a similar amount of design time to them as any other area in the project. The same underlying design principles apply here. Incorporating a thoughtfully designed outdoor space into your co-living HMO project will help attract more tenant enquiries and retain housemates longer, which will maximise your ROI.

If your co-living HMO has a large garden, why not consider installing a garden cabin as a multi-use space? Timber-frame structures can be insulated, hooked up to the electrics and fitted out as a yoga space, gym, office or private snug.

Cinema rooms

With large TVs in café kitchens, customers are able to catch up on the news, short programmes and sports over breakfast, lunch or dinner. While casual TV watching is reserved for the café kitchens, Netflix binges are more suited to a dedicated cinema room. These spaces encourage movie nights, which bring the community together.

Cinema rooms do not need any natural light, so basements or internal spaces with no other use are ideal. This can be a good consideration when you are at the architectural layout stage.

Casual bean-bag seating is more flexible than formal sofas and allows the customer to re-arrange and personalise the space. For the equipment, you can choose either oversized HD TVs or ceiling-mounted projectors with wide-angle lenses, but one of the benefits of projectors is that when they're not in use, the space can be re-purposed as a fitness room or quiet study.

Fitness space

Although you don't necessarily need to create dedicated gyms, you could design breakout and outdoor spaces to be multi-purpose so that they can be reconfigured for fitness use. In larger co-living HMO developments, though, it is not uncommon to see dedicated gyms with a range of fitness equipment such as running machines, rowing machines, free weights and stretching areas. Similar to cinema rooms, these spaces do not always require natural light, so you can make use of internal areas within the building. Yoga and small fitness classes can also utilise the open-plan gym space.

Co-working and workspace

Although you may provide desks in bedrooms, these are not ideal for long periods of work. As an experiment, my company created dedicated multi-use co-working rooms with large bench seating to see how the spaces would be used by the customers. This first co-working space was so successful, we have since rolled them out to other sites and had positive feedback. Many customers who work from home value a dedicated workspace away from the main community space in the building.

When you're designing co-working spaces, consider technology from the outset. Make sure there are plenty of desk-height power points, along with large desks, workshop space, comfortable ergonomic chairs, large wall-mounted displays for second screen use, whiteboards and a range of lighting options.

The way we work is changing and more people are moving to a flexible work arrangement. Using the Co-Living Innovation Canvas and the Space Design Blueprint, you can create your own range of workspace areas.

Bedroom design

Within co-living HMOs, the bedroom is your customer's private space away from the hustle and bustle of community life. When you're designing a co-living HMO bedroom, consider factors such as size, layout, comfort, storage, personalisation, feature walls and headboards, project desks, mood lighting, tech and heating.

Size

The space you have available for your bedrooms may impact your design decisions and layout options. Many co-living projects feature a range of bedroom sizes, which will reflect in the different rents you charge for each room. It's important to learn how to design small spaces for this purpose as well as larger ones (more on this coming up in the 'Layout' section).

Bedrooms can range from smaller than 10 sqm up to larger than 20 sqm spaces. I find I can rent out larger rooms first as people tend to value more space and are happy to pay more for this. I challenge myself with every new project to source buildings with the scope for developing large bedrooms.

Layout

The way you design a small bedroom will be different to the way you design a larger one. For example, in a small bedroom, the bed will almost certainly be located in a corner to increase the available floor space. In larger rooms, you may locate a bed centrally on a feature wall. It is a good idea to locate the bed away from the hallway wall to minimise any sound from the busy communal areas.

An important tip is to make sure you locate aerial points and the TV opposite the bed if possible. Unless you include a separate sofa or armchair in the bedroom, the housemate will want to watch TV while sitting up in bed, so reflect this need in the layout from the outset of the design process.

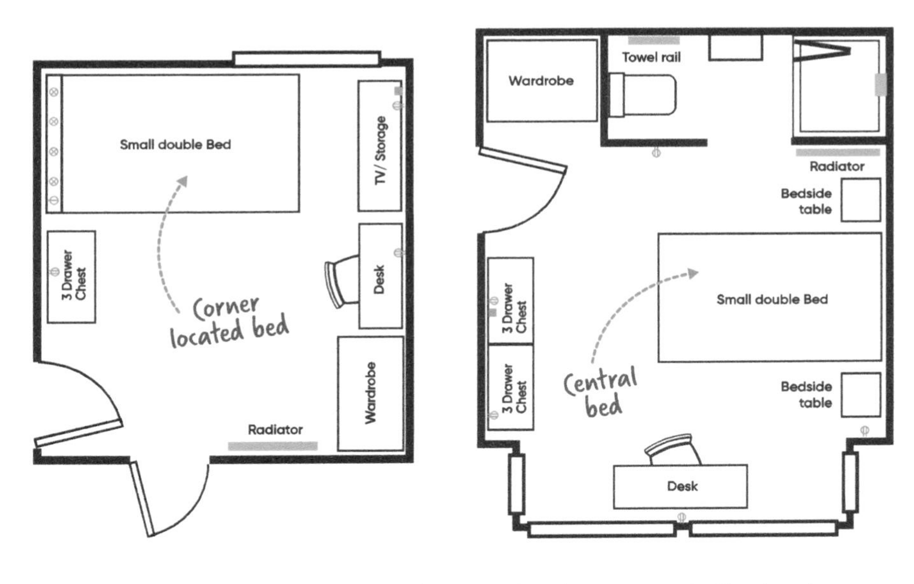

These floorplans show the difference in layout options between central bed and corner bed positioning. In smaller rooms, placing a bed in the corner leaves more visible carpet space when the customer enters the bedroom, which will feel more spacious as a result.

Comfort

When you're designing a co-living HMO bedroom, comfort is a key factor in creating a good experience. One of the best ways to ensure your customers' comfort is to invest in a good-quality mattress, such as pocket sprung with memory foam upper. This is a technique we took from our aparthotels where we were advised to invest in the best mattresses we could buy. This investment directly impacts a positive customer experience.

Dependent on the size of the room, install mattresses that are either 4 foot or 4 foot 6 wide. Include blackout blinds as standard in all bedrooms to help housemates get a good night's sleep.

Storage

My approach to bedroom storage is to provide a lot more than the standard HMO allowance. In general, HMOs include a small wardrobe, a chest of drawers and a bedside cabinet. Can you imagine getting all your possessions into these three pieces of furniture?

You only have to conduct a property inspection to see how much stuff housemates bring with them. Early research by my company indicated that we needed to increase the volume of bedroom storage, and now all our rooms feature a wardrobe with two drawers, multiple chests of drawers (which double up as TV stands), open bookcase storage, a desk, shelves, hooks and bedside tables.

Personalisation

One way to help housemates feel at home is to provide space for personalisation within the bedroom. There is an opportunity at the design stage to add areas that allow housemates to decorate the space with pictures of family and friends and posters of their interests.

There are many techniques you can use to allow customers to personalise a space, but the two I favour are pegboards and picture shelves. Plywood pegboards can be custom built by your carpenter to fit spaces in the bedroom, such as wall areas, or as part of project desks.

If you are upgrading existing HMOs, you can buy pegboards ready-made online and get them installed by a handy person. Another option for personalisation is a picture shelf above the bed with a range of frames that the housemate can fill with their own pictures.

Feature walls and headboards

I always invest in at least one feature wall within a bedroom, usually the wall directly behind the bed. Using a range of techniques, from simple wallpaper through to complex timber panelling, I create a dramatic centrepiece within the room. Over the years, I have experimented with a number of materials and design styles, in many cases blending them with mood lighting.

Feature walls can be the headboard of the bed. Alternatively, you can create an additional headboard with integrated lighting and phone charging. On our Co-Living Mastermind we share the construction techniques and key suppliers to help landlords create their own bedroom designs, feature walls and bespoke headboards similar to the photos shared in this book.

Examples of our co-living HMO bedrooms

FLEX
DELL

Project desk

Dependent on the size of the bedroom, you may have space for a project desk. In larger rooms, this can be a core feature.

We have already discussed how co-working and breakout spaces are important so that housemates do not have to spend all their time in their bedrooms. If space is at a premium and you do not have an area for dedicated co-working, then it is a good idea to integrate a project desk into the bedrooms. A project desk is a table, usually 1 m wide with storage, shelving and personalisation areas. I call them 'project desks' rather than workstations as they are designed for personal life projects and casual use as opposed to long periods of work.

Lighting

Provide multiple mood-lighting options within the bedroom so the customer can choose how to set the feel of the space. Dependent on your budget, these can range from custom light-emitting diode (LED) headboards and dimmable cluster lights through to simple bedside drop pendants or floor lamps.

If you are providing a project station in the bedroom, this will need dedicated task lighting. I label all lighting on the second-fix plans and provide these in a design appendix to my electrician (we will discuss this in Chapter 11).

Technology

When it comes to technology in the bedroom space, consider a few basics. You will need at least three double sockets, their position based on your design layout, and the height of these sockets will be dependent on the furniture. For example, if you are putting sockets where a chest of drawers is located, then positioning these at a height of 90 cm will allow easy access.

Make sure that one of the double sockets, usually the one near the bed, also has USB sockets for easy device charging. Custom headboards generally feature USB points for mobile phone charging similar to those you would find in hotel rooms as customers tend to like to keep their phone close to the bed. Consider the location of the TV aerial from the outset and make sure there's a suitable position opposite the bed for the TV. Wi-fi signal in the bedroom needs to be strong (we will cover this in the upcoming section on support and technology).

Heating

When I design co-living HMO bedrooms, the radiator is the last thing I put in position on the floorplans. As modern radiators are highly efficient, they can be positioned anywhere in the bedroom, so first of all, I work on the layout of the bed, storage, desk and lighting. This then informs the best location for a radiator.

What you want to avoid is having to design the whole room around a radiator. Given the competitive price of radiators, you can probably afford to put in efficient modern versions with thermostatic radiator valves. If space is limited, you may even decide to use vertical radiators.

10 sqm bedroom with door and radiator changes

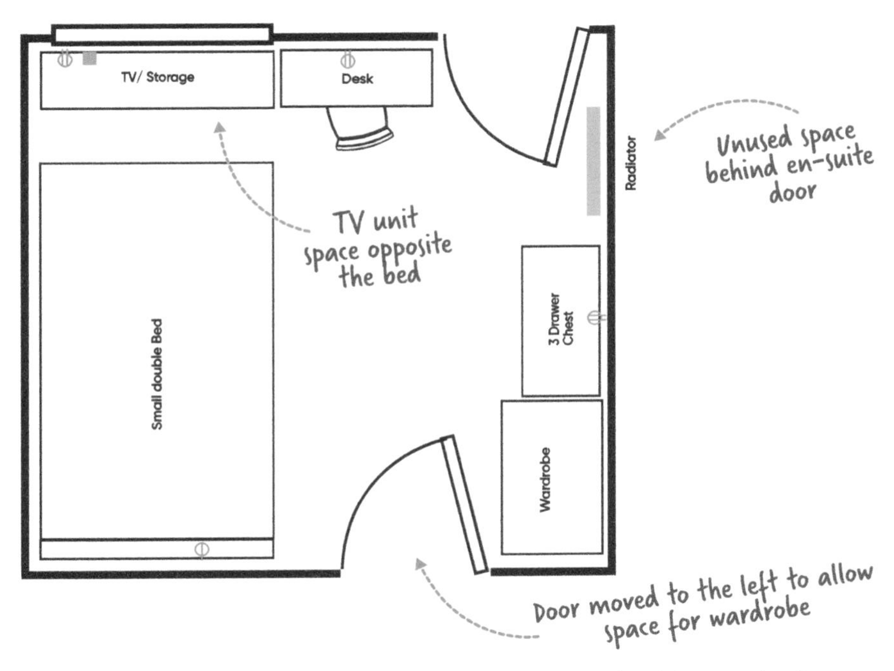

This floorplan shows how the radiator has been positioned behind the en-suite door so as not to impact on the TV unit space or storage in a 10 sqm room. Moving the entrance door slightly ensured the wardrobe fitted in the corner.

Private spaces

Access to a range of private spaces is integral to enhancing customers' wellbeing and relaxation when they're residing in a co-living community. Private spaces can be more than just a bedroom; they also include bathrooms, breakout spaces and small private nooks. A combination of private and semi-private spaces gives your customers options on how they want to live, and this personalisation will help create a balanced experience for them.

Private breakout spaces and nooks

We spoke earlier about breakout spaces and how they can be multi-use. Within the context of private space, they really come into their own. Outside of your customer's bedroom, they provide a secluded space for them to relax, read a book or maybe work alone.

The most important part of this concept is that these spaces are in addition and separate to the main social space. Giving housemates the option of how to use a space allows them more personalisation, which in turn will lead to better occupancy.

Private nooks are tiny spaces, sometimes only big enough for one person, that are tucked into corners. Examples include small reading nooks, sun loungers and outdoor hammock zones. Get creative and think how you can repurpose unused space in your property.

Bathrooms

The subject of private bathrooms comes up many times and landlords often debate it at length. There are a number of options available here: shared bathrooms, en-suites and off-suites. En-suites are located within the bedroom whereas off-suites are located close to the bedroom, but accessed from the hallway. When I create shared bathrooms, I look to use a ratio of two housemates to one bathroom. Any more sharing a bathroom would not be easy to sell to potential new housemates.

There are four key considerations when you're deciding on bathrooms as part of your project:

- **Budget**. There is a cost to installing new bathrooms, so your decision comes down to your overall numbers and the deal stack.
- **The building** may only feasibly fit in a certain number of bathrooms, dependent on the footprint, services and layout. Work with an architect to assess this at the outset.
- **Customer insight** will highlight how important a private bathroom is to your target demographics.
- **Local market.** Every market is different and en-suites are not required everywhere. This is where it pays to understand your target area.

In the South-East, my company's research has found that housemates would ideally not want to share a bathroom if given a choice, but they are not bothered if the bathroom door is off the hallway as long as the room is private. In a competitive market, rooms with access to private bathrooms achieve higher rents and sell faster than those with a shared bathroom.

When you're designing the shower space, install a combination of waterfall above and hand-held shower attachments. Such a small difference in the cost will make for a much better shower experience for your housemates. I'm sure you can remember having a bad shower, perhaps in a hotel room. Put yourself in the customer's shoes and think which small details will make for a great day.

Don't forget to make a note of all your sanitary ware suppliers and model numbers so that you can order spares for any future maintenance.

Support and technology

Alongside social, co-working and private spaces, co-living HMOs require a whole range of support facilities and technology. In this section, we will discuss superfast mesh wi-fi, unvented heating systems and plant rooms, smart controls, multi-zone mood lighting, cleaning services, laundry space and bike storage.

Superfast mesh wi-fi

Everything in your co-living HMO could stop working, but when the internet goes down, you will hear about it within seconds. People today tend to be hyper-connected, so your customers' ability to access wi-fi is non-negotiable. They expect superfast internet speeds and a stable connection throughout the day. With customers streaming content, working remotely and socialising on the internet, you need to have a strategy in place provide a great service on this.

On every one of your projects, specify the internet infrastructure and layout at the design stage. Firstly, the feed into the building needs to be the fastest you can get.

The next hurdle to overcome is wi-fi coverage. I'm sure at some point, you have experienced low signal issues when your router is at one end of the house and you are at the other. Standard routers are not powerful enough to provide sufficient signal quality across multiple floors and large floorplan layouts, so install additional wi-fi boosters across the building to ensure 100% signal everywhere. This means your customer can always get a strong, stable internet connection at any time of the day and on any floor of the building. This upfront investment pays dividends by improving the overall experience.

Unvented heating and plant room

You will need to consider the heating system from the outset. The objective is to ensure every housemate can access a hot shower and heating without any issues. It will annoy them if the water goes cold while they're showering or they only get a trickle out of the shower head, but you can design the infrastructure upfront to mitigate this happening. Once this is in place, you can replicate the specification in ongoing projects.

Generally speaking, up to three showers in a property can use a high-spec combi boiler system. If you add a fourth bathroom into the property, you could introduce a single electric shower. For properties with five or more bathrooms, I recommend an unvented cylinder system. This will consist of a large storage tank, expansion vessel, pipework and boiler. Unvented systems don't rely on gravity so can maintain consistent pressure and be located anywhere in the property.

Given the large amount of equipment required for an unvented cylinder system, you will need to create a dedicated plant room in the building. There are a huge range of tank sizes available, dependent on the number of bathrooms you are servicing, but don't worry – you don't need to dedicate a whole bedroom to this. You can carve an area off a larger room, kitchen or hallway to accommodate the boiler and cylinder tanks.

If you have an unused loft area, you may consider horizontal tanks rather than vertical. However, it is good practice to consider where to site the tank at the outset. It is often overlooked.

SP

Multi-zone mood lighting

To improve the co-living HMO experience, install a selection of lighting types. I have experimented with a wide range, from dimmable, LED, back and cluster lighting to more complex conduit lighting patterns.

One of my company's signature styles is the use of lighting clusters. I learned this technique many years ago when working with the renowned UK lighting designer Tom Dixon. When combined with dimmable switches, this creates a dramatic controllable lighting effect.

Using a range of lighting types, you can completely transform any space. When you're designing your co-living HMO, the best time to consider and explore lighting is during the first-fix design stage (see Chapter 11).

Smart controls

If you are renting to professionals, then the chances are you will include the bills in a single rent payment. Given you will be paying for all the utilities, it makes sense to be energy efficient from the outset. One of the common problems in co-living HMOs is that housemates will crank up the heating, then forget to turn it down again. When you multiply this by several housemates, you risk high energy usage across your portfolio.

Thermostats that improve energy efficiency by providing a generous heating pattern across weekdays and weekends work well to mitigate this risk. Housemates can increase the temperature or boost the heating as much as they want, but after two hours, the system will automatically re-adjust to the set pattern. If the pattern requires any adjustment based on usage, you can login remotely and adjust it at a click of a button.

There are now smart sensors you can add to the system to detect humidity, motion and temperature. Using technology in this way, you will allow your property to adjust the settings automatically. Now that is smart!

Cleaning services

Over the years, co-living HMOs have moved closer to the hospitality model where operators provide almost a concierge service to customers. My advice would be to book a regular cleaner, who visits every two weeks to clean the social spaces, hallways and any shared bathrooms, and a separate handy person who cleans and tends to the outdoor spaces. Any private spaces, such as bedrooms and en-suites, are outside the cleaner's remit, but you can give housemates the option to upgrade to having their bedrooms and en-suites cleaned if they require it.

Don't forget to allow some storage space in case cleaners need to keep supplies of cleaning products or equipment onsite. Also remember to add a socket on every hallway floor for the cleaners to use.

Laundry space

Dependent on the size of your co-living HMO, you will have either a laundry area or a dedicated laundry room. One thing to consider with washing machines and tumble dryers is that they will get a lot of use, so it is worth investing in decent models with low energy costs.

When you're designing the laundry space or room, think about appliance positioning. They will create noise and you will want to minimise disturbance to housemates. If you are limited on space, a good tip is to stack devices so tumble dryers can sit on top of washing machines. With tumble dryers, vented would be better, but if they are not located against an outside wall, then condensing versions are fine.

A key consideration with a laundry space is vibration. It is advisable to keep the laundry equipment on the ground floor if possible. Even if you use anti-vibration pads, it is amazing how far low-level vibrations can travel in a building if a washing machine is installed on upper floors.

A single large-capacity washing machine and separate tumble dryer are sufficient for six sharers. If you develop sui generis HMOs, look to add multiple appliances.

Bike storage

As part of promoting a healthy lifestyle, support bike usage for housemates who are commuting to work. When you're designing outdoor spaces, integrate dedicated bike store areas into either landscaped gardens, patios or building frontage.

When your architect draws up the building plans, ask them to include the garden and key dimensions. At the design stage, model options on these plans for bike racks to be installed by the builder or handy person. This is a great selling feature when people view the property as many will be wondering where will they store their bikes. These days, many bikes are worth a lot of money, so safe, lockable storage is a good facility to offer.

When you're designing bike stores, don't forget to upgrade the garden gate lock to allow key access from the exterior. Many old gates only have internal locking, which is no good if your customers want to bring their bikes straight in from the back of the property.

Summary

In this chapter, we have covered how you can use the Space Design Blueprint to design a range of inspiring spaces to improve the customer's living experience. We've discussed how you can create amazing social spaces, including café kitchen, breakout, co-working, cinema and landscaped outdoor areas. You now know how to design bedrooms and bathrooms that optimise space and provide comfort.

With technology evolving so rapidly, you need to integrate superfast mesh wi-fi, efficient heating systems, smart controls and mood lighting into your co-living HMO. The Space Design Blueprint will help you with all this and more so you can deliver a high-quality product to the market that will both attract enquiries and increase occupancy as housemates stay.

Find out how Bronwen secured two properties to convert into co-living HMOs in just six months. After she'd implemented the direct-to-vendor deal sourcing technique and dealt with a range of setbacks, her perseverance paid off. With a combination of Bronwen's love of design and the Space Design Masterclasses on my company's mastermind, she is now confidently creating her own co-living HMOs and property brand.

To watch the full video visit
www.theco-livingrevolution.co.uk/mastermind

BUILD & LEARN

After you have secured your site and put a plan in place to transform the building, the next step is to deliver the end product. It can be daunting managing extensive refurbishment works, but with the right systems and processes in place, you can significantly reduce the risk.

As a developer, your objective is to deliver the project successfully, on time and on budget, so you will require documentation to build to the specification you want. As co-living HMOs are design-led, this will mean you require a detailed specification. Dependent on the size of your building works, you may be working with many tradespeople who will be looking to you for guidance and answers when problems come up during the build.

In this chapter, we will look at the process you need to follow to ensure that you can deliver your co-living HMO projects successfully time after time. We will then look at how you can gather and use data from your projects and customers to learn, adapt and improve.

Managing the build

In this section, we will discuss the process to ensure you can successfully build and deliver your co-living HMOs. The stages of this process are:

- Create tender packs
- Create architect's plans and SOW
- Create SOW appendix
- Create design and first-fix appendix
- Use sketches and visuals
- Manage variations and extras
- Project management and snagging

Tender packs

Even if you have a number of contractors you use regularly, it is important to put projects out to tender. This way, you are continually expanding your contractor database to ensure you can secure the most competitive price. This database of trusted tradespeople will become a valuable asset as you move towards working on co-living HMO developments concurrently.

Your tender pack for every project needs to contain a number of key documents:

- Architect's plans (multiple docs)
- Architect's SOW
- SOW appendix/design and first-fix appendix
- Steel calculations (organised by your architect)
- Asbestos survey (you will need to find a local company for this prior to any works starting as your builder will want to know the site is safe)

Make sure all documents have version numbers and page numbers as they may change or get out of order when onsite.

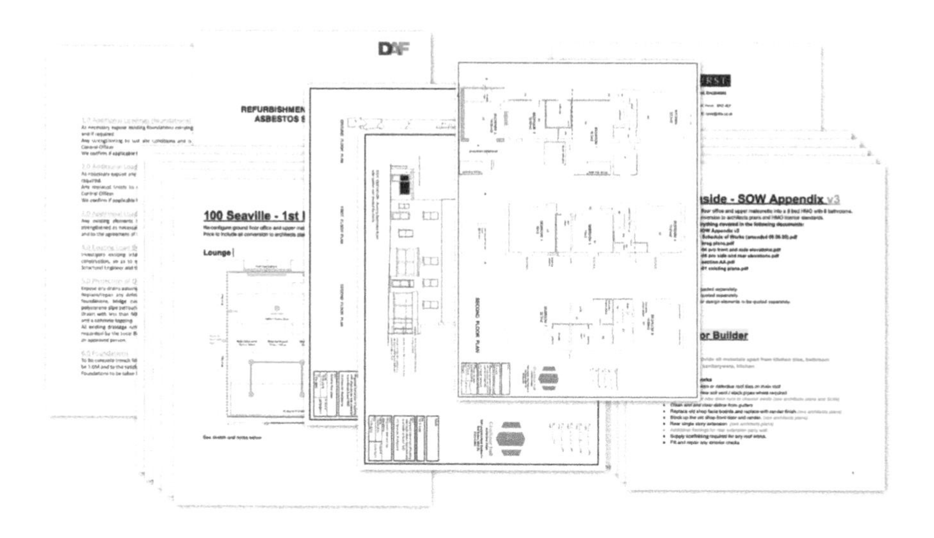

Architect's plans and SOW

One of the first things to do after securing a deal off the market is to get the floorplans drawn up by an architect. Instruct the architect as soon as the deal is agreed so that you can start the design phase during conveyancing. Given it will take time for the architect to get to site and draw up the plans, it pays to book this in early.

At the architectural design stage, your focus is on transforming the building to provide the spaces you'll need for a co-living HMO. Refer to the Space Design Blueprint in Chapter 10 for more information on the range of spaces possible. The architect's initial plans will not design the final bedroom interiors or social space layouts; they will just focus on rooms and volume. You will already have an idea of what is possible with the site, but this phase will explore options to increase the number of rooms (density) or look at other creative angles to improve the layout.

Once you are happy you have maximised the development opportunity within the site and ensured the numbers stack (very important), the next stage is to get more detailed on the internal layout. Use the plans to test a number of internal layouts as you may find that moving a door or other simple adjustments will make all the difference.

It is at this stage that you need to consider where you'll put furniture and sockets into the space so you can optimise the layout before adding plans to the tender pack. This can be done by your architect, or you could do it yourself using a range of low-cost online floor-planner apps. Once this test is complete, it forms your draft internal layout to ensure the tender pack is as accurate as possible. Your architect will then produce a set of building regulations plans along with a SOW that will form part of your tender pack.

SOW appendix

When you're designing co-living HMOs, it is important to capture as much information as possible in the initial brief to the contractor. This extra work up front will minimise variations (extras) on the back end, so it pays to spend time on this stage.

The architect will create the floorplans, elevations and SOW, but these will not contain key information on first fix (ie electrical socket and plumbing requirements), second-fix fit out (ie kitchen design, layout, feature walls, bespoke work) and finishing. Any quotes you gather via tendering have to include all works listed in the architect's plans, SOW and SOW appendix. The last thing you want is the dreaded conversation with a contractor when they start adding items that were not included, so make it clear from the outset that you only want quotes that cover everything on the listed documents and highlight any exclusions.

The SOW appendix covers these areas in more detail:

- Exterior, remedial and insulation works
- General building works
- New glazing and doors required
- Room-by-room breakdown with architect's floor plans
- Allowance for number of sockets, lighting and plumbing requirements per room
- Allowance for boiler, plant room, towel rails, radiators and bathrooms
- Allowance for any feature wall materials based on basic sqm coverage
- Visual reference to any trade-supplied products such as fire doors, handle styles, sanitary ware, socket styles etc
- Guide to HMO requirements
- Allowance for tiling requirement
- Allowance for painting and decorating

SOW appendix documents are separated by trade, eg builder, plumber and electrician. You can source areas such as flooring and UPVC glazing directly yourself to find better deals. Work with either a single contractor who will provide everything or a builder who will introduce a plumber and electrician. A SOW appendix that is separated by trade will make their lives easier when it comes to quoting.

Design and first-fix appendix

In most cases, you will not have fully designed the rooms when you send out the tender, so you will need to make allowances for materials, wall finishes and sockets. Once the quote is signed off, you can follow up with a more detailed design and first-fix appendix. The SOW appendix and the design and first-fix appendix documents can be either combined or separate, dependent on how much time you have before tendering the project. In most cases I get the SOW appendix quoted by the contractor and then provide a more detailed design and first fix appendix after the project has begun. The SOW appendix is based on allowances (ie number of sockets, radiators and feature walls) so this should be reasonably accurate prior to your renovation starting.

The design and first-fix appendix covers these areas in more detail:

- Room-by-room breakdown with close up floor plans showing locations of all first-fix items such as plumbing and electrical (with key measurements)
- Location of boiler, plant room, towel rails and radiators, and bathroom layouts
- Layout and location of any feature walls
- Guide to any bespoke work with sketches or mock-ups
- Tiling guide with locations, visual reference and pattern layout
- Painting and decorating guide with colour references

There is a chance you may update the floorplans once the project has started. The important thing in this instance is to submit a new design and first-fix appendix with updated floorplans and description, and a version number on the document. You will then need to discuss the revision with the contractor to see if there are any extras outside the initial scope. Any chargeable changes can then be added to the central extras list you agree.

Sketches and visuals

Visuals are a great way to indicate how something will look before it exists. These only have to be rough with just enough detail to explain what needs to be built. Visuals can range from simple sketches and annotations over photos to more complex overlays on architectural floorplans.

There are a number of different visuals to include in the SOW appendix:

- Layout of first-fix items (electrical and plumbing)
- Feature wall locations and supporting sketches
- Tiling guides/patterns
- Bespoke lighting plans or sketches
- Sketches of 3D room views

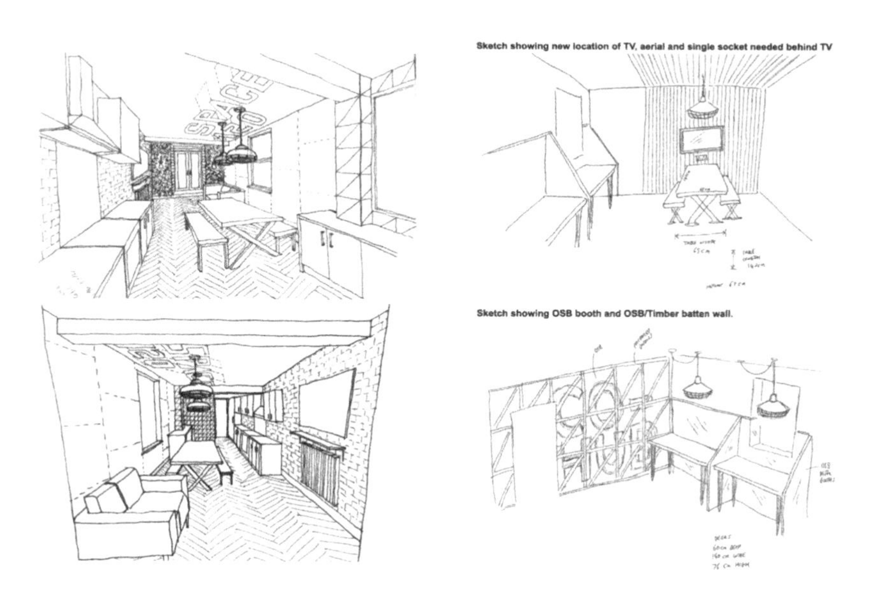

Sketch showing new location of TV, aerial and single socket needed behind TV

Sketch showing OSB booth and OSB/Timber batten wall.

Manage variations and extras

To keep close to budget, you will need to be on top of variations and extras as the cost can increase rapidly without management. Allow around 5–10% of your budget as contingency for extras, dependent on the scale of the project.

Make it clear to contractors at the start of the project that you will only pay for extras or changes that are quoted and signed off. I manage this by creating a dedicated spreadsheet (yes, another one!) for any extras I've agreed with contractors and adding it to the building contract so there is no confusion later. If you're working with contractors who are more tech savvy, you may sometimes share access to the variations and extras spreadsheet so they can enter any items for you to provide sign off.

Project management and snagging

Your choice of project management will depend on the scale of your co-living HMO project and the number of concurrent projects you have on the go. If you are new to developments and located near to your site, it's good to get involved in the project management yourself.

It is important for you to understand the build process by working closely with tradespeople. Working regularly onsite, you will learn how to speak their language and about remedial issues, structural works and extensions, which will make it much easier for you to create SOW documents in future. This knowledge can also be useful when you're viewing potential sites as you will recognise problems such as damp or structural issues and be able to visualise how to modify the building and the number of rooms possible.

If you are working on multiple projects, large buildings or sites located far from your home, I would recommend hiring a freelance project manager. As long as your tender pack and SOW appendix are detailed enough, you will be able to hand your project over to someone else to manage on a day-to-day basis.

Prior to release of the contractors' final payment, you have an opportunity to go round the site and create a snagging list. It is worth spending some time on this as it is better to identify any problems while the build team is still onsite. Follow a checklist in every room and don't rush this process as it pays to spot the small details. You can use apps that allow you to take pictures and make notes while onsite, and then email a report to the builders.

Learn, adapt and improve

After the fit out is complete and you have launched your first co-living HMO on to the market, you need to capture and measure data and learn from it. Your first project is essentially a collection of experiments that require feedback. Over time, you will gather valuable insight into what works and areas for improvement.

In this section, we will explore the value of data to your co-living HMO business and how it can supercharge your developments. We will discuss techniques to gather data from all corners of your property business and how to use that data to learn and adapt.

The value of data

One of the most valuable returns from your co-living HMO business is data. In a world that is hyper-connected and technology driven, data is the new gold dust. The quality and quantity of the data you gather can have a direct impact on your ability to create a better product, outperform the market and stay one step ahead of competitors.

Big data is here to stay. It plays an important part in elections, social media and marketing. Just as your database of leads and potential investors is valuable, you also need to treat business data as a strategic asset. Once you have data, you can use it to inform your product design, customer experience and marketing.

Gathering data

Gather data from as many areas as possible across each stage of the co-living customer journey, then centralise it on the cloud so you can access it easily and review it when you're starting your next design phase. Here are just a few areas to capture data from:

- Product launches create data across physical, digital and social media on enquiries, demand, feedback and sales.

- Websites hooked up to Google Analytics can analyse search data and how this can inform future marketing of your spaces.
- Centralise housemate application data on the cloud so you can access it to analyse trends such as age groups, job types, demand and interests.
- Run gorilla research user surveys within your community of housemates to gather feedback on your spaces (product) and their experience.

As you can see, the amount of data you can capture is endless. It's worth noting that many landlords are not even thinking about this, so gathering and storing data is a great way to get ahead of your competition. The most important thing to remember is to centralise the data you capture so it is easily accessible to inform business decisions.

Using data

The beauty of capturing rich data in your business is that it feeds back into new products and experiences. It is this continual loop of learning and refinement that drives innovation. The objective is to analyse the data you gather, looking for trends that feed back into your product and marketing. Knowing who your customers are and what they want can transform your co-living HMO business and your revenue.

This focus on customer centric design will lead to high occupancy, high rents and increased customer satisfaction.

The data you capture in your business can be used to improve:

- Marketing, advertising and brand message
- New ideas and product innovation
- Customer experience and satisfaction
- Use of technology and processes
- Overall portfolio performance
- Ongoing strategy for growth

Summary

With co-living HMOs, you need detailed specifications to ensure your build team can successfully deliver the end product. In this chapter, we have discussed how to create a tendering pack for contractors and the importance of an SOW appendix to capture design information. Once the build has started, we covered the role of a project manager, minimising extra costs and capturing any snagging issues early.

Data is vitally important to any business, so we finished this chapter (and this part on 'Product') by looking at the ways you can gather it and how to use it to inform your business decisions so you can create a great product and experience.

Great product + great experience = happy customers.

Bonus Content

Visit **www.theco-livingrevolution.co.uk/bonus**
for your free content, checklists and resources to help you get started on your co-living HMO journey.

After attending many general property courses, Rudi decided to gain more specific co-living HMO knowledge and deal-stacking support. Find out how Rudi went from a standing start to secure her first property and utilise tender packs and SOW appendix templates (provided on the Co-Living Mastermind™) to confidently work with builders.

To watch the full video visit
www.theco-livingrevolution.co.uk/mastermind

PART FOUR _
BRAND, COMMUNITY, EXPERIENCE, & SCALE

ATTRACTION

In a world of hyper-connected customers and digital technology, landlords are needing their own property brands to stand out from the crowd. This approach allows you to build trust and loyalty with potential customers, just like your favourite lifestyle brands do.

Creating your own property brand will help you convey your mission, your values and your product. Would you like to attract new opportunities and investors? Would you like a stream of enquires from people wanting to live in your co-living HMOs? If you get this right, it will create attraction marketing for you.

In this section, we are going to be covering the Build a Brand model, which includes the concept of customer touchpoints, developing your brand identity and mission, creating a suite of brand assets, branding your co-living HMO space, the importance of having a digital presence, and utilising social media to expand your reach.

Build a brand model

The concept of customer touchpoints

Before we dive into marketing techniques, one of the most important concepts I want to share with you is customer touchpoints. As people engage with any brand, they are doing so across a range of both digital and physical environments, from social media posts and TV adverts to products in physical stores and at events. Your investors and potential housemates will go through exactly the same process. It is by identifying this range of touchpoints that you can improve the customer journey.

Google has done some fascinating research into touchpoints and created a model called Zero Moment Of Truth (ZMOT).[22] It refers to the moment at which a customer reaches the decision to buy. Google found that buyers need to spend approximately seven hours viewing content across eleven touchpoints in four locations before they will buy.

If you apply this same thinking to your co-living HMO business, it highlights the importance of creating a range of brand assets covering physical and digital.

Develop your brand identity and mission

Your company mission statement will answer three key questions: what you do, who you do it for and how you do it. Once you have created your mission statement, you can then present it front and centre across your website and marketing as a powerful message so all your customers know the reason why you do what you do. Essentially, your mission statement gets to the heart of why your brand exists and what it stands for.

Your mission statement drives your business towards your goal and helps articulate your purpose to your power team and potential customers. Here are a couple of examples of company mission statements:

- **Nike** – 'To bring inspiration and innovation to every athlete in the world'.[23]
- **LinkedIn** – 'To connect the world's professionals to make them more productive and successful.'[24]

You may find you mission statement goes through a few iterations as you swap words for more impactful alternatives. This is fine – it's all part of the process.

Creating your own brand identity will help your property business stand out within the HMO market. As a developer and landlord, you need a customer-facing brand to drive new business. Before potential housemates or investors meet you or visit one of your properties, they

YOUR PRODUCT IS PART OF YOUR BRAND

THE CO-LIVING REVOLUTION™

may research your brand and read some of your content. In a fast-moving technology-driven world, the customer expects to engage with memorable brands that align with their values.

When designing your brand, you are looking to create a style or personality that conveys what you stand for. Your brand is a powerful medium to convey your values and mission. We have talked about the importance of getting the edge in business. Your brand is an essential part of your co-living HMO business as it gives you an edge in the market.

To help create your own brand's look, I recommend you contact local graphic design freelancers or agencies. Have a look at their portfolios and select a company whose style of work you like.

A few of our brands

our development and operations company

one of our self service boutique hotels in Brighton

our core mentoring programme for landlords

Create a suite of brand assets

As you develop your own brand, you will build a number of key assets. What started as a simple logo, colours and typography will expand to printed physical items and digital content.

There is a whole range of brand assets, but let's start with the basic ones that you will need as you grow your co-living HMO business:

- **Logo** – your suite of logo files covering different file types (ie JPG, EPS, PNG) and variations (ie colour logo, BW logo, logo on transparent background).
- **Fonts** – a central folder of the brand fonts that can be loaded on any computer. Your designer will provide these files for you.
- **Stationery** – business cards are a key networking asset, so they need to encourage contacts to visit your website. A clear call to action would be to feature your website address on these cards.
- **Investor pack** – prepared for potential investors so they can find out more about your brand, your mission and your range of services. These can be distributed as PDF files for convenience.
- **Artwork** – custom graphics prepared for your co-living spaces. These could include designs for picture frames, vinyl graphics for doors and hallways and custom murals for feature walls.

Brand your co-living HMO space

The important thing to remember with a brand is that it exists everywhere in your business, and this includes the physical product itself. It may seem odd to discuss the product as part of your brand, but your brand identity comes to life in your product.

When you are creating co-living HMOs, incorporate your brand into the space as part of the design process. There is a journey every customer makes from seeing your brand online, exploring your website, viewing adverts, to attending viewings and living in the space itself. Your brand is represented at every stage of the customer journey and that is why the quality of your product is so important.

As you develop your brand, you will be able to take key elements (logos, typography, illustrations, images, colours, styles) and translate them into the physical spaces you create. I call this branding your space. Take a Dyson vacuum cleaner, for example. Everything about the construction and product style feels like a Dyson. The workmanship and end product represent the brand. That same workmanship and product design then flow into packaging, marketing and advertising.

As you build out your first co-living HMO, you will create a style that will evolve. Adding design features such as custom artwork, colour and graphics will allow you to add a brand layer to the space. This is all part of finding you unique brand style.

A good way to brand your space is through wayfinding and artwork. Wayfinding is a visual language (signs and directions) throughout the building to indicate where things are via the use of icons, illustrations and typography. You see this a lot in public spaces such as airports, city centres and attractions. Not only does this add a layer of brand identity, but it also helps housemates and guests orientate themselves in the building. Artwork can take the form of photos, murals, vinyl graphics and graffiti which can transform a space by adding an extra brand layer.

The importance of having a digital presence

Having a digital presence is vital in today's always connected world. Your customers (both investors and housemates) are likely to spend most of their time online, so tapping into the digital world is essential for building your brand exposure.

People may meet you in person or hear of your company via word of mouth, but at some point, they will look for you online. Don't worry – you don't have to become a digital expert or be prolific across all channels; you just need to build up your digital assets and ensure a consistency of brand across all of them. Think of these assets as additional touchpoints – the more touchpoints customers see on their journey, the more likely they are to buy from you.

Here are a few digital assets you will need as you grow:

- **Website** – keep this simple; it does not need to be a multi-page monster. A few pages about you, your mission, what you offer, your projects and contact details will suffice.
- **Email footers** – this will add a layer of professionalism for your customers. Customise the footer with your logo, contact details, links to website, social channels and any news.
- **Email newsletters** – one of the first things I would recommend doing when you build your website is to set up a pop-up data-capture form asking visitors if they would like to join your newsletter, as this will build your database.
- **PDF content** – make sure your printed brochures and investor packs exist as PDFs so they can be easily emailed.
- **Photoshoot images** – once you have created your first co-living HMO, pay for a professional photoshoot. These images will help sell the rooms on your website, social media and marketing.
- **Social media profile pages** – love it or loathe it, social media is an important part of running a business. You customers are on these channels, so it's important to have a presence and be visible on them.

Utilise social media to expand your reach

The subject of social media could fill a whole book on its own. Here, I'll just give you a high-level view of how to use it for your business and some simple techniques to get you started.

Social media is like a vast networking space where you can socialise with other people regardless of geographical location. As a property developer, you will expand your reach and your network by being on social media, providing you with an additional stream of enquiries and business opportunities.

Here are a few ways you can get started:

- Focus on a small number of social channels and build up slowly over time.
- Set up your profile/business pages so that you have a presence on your chosen channels. If you have already created your basic website, then use some of the images and copy from that.
- When posting on social media, be authentic. Be yourself.
- Try to respond and engage with anyone who comments on your posts.

To avoid overwhelm, only commit to a manageable amount of regular posts on social media. You may start with one post a week, then add more in the future. It's about consistency rather than volume.

You might be wondering what you can say every week. How do you come up with new posts? I was given some great advice many years ago which was to simply document my journey. Every week, take photos of everything you do such as visiting sites, searching for properties, looking at floorplans and travelling. You're always likely to have your phone to hand, so take as many photos as you can. At the end of the week, look back at the images and pick out a few key ones that describe what you have been doing.

Summary

In this chapter, we have covered the third step of the SPACES model: attraction. How do you attract your ideal customer, be they housemates for your co-living HMOs or potential investors?

The answer is that you utilise attraction marketing to take your property business to the next level, which means putting the Build a Brand model into practice. The model includes:

- Identifying and increasing the number of touchpoints your brand is featured across
- Your mission statement and brand identity, and how these are powerful tools to attract enquiries
- Building your suite of brand assets for future marketing
- How to brand your physical spaces
- Top tips on creating your digital presence and content
- Why the use of social media can help expand your network

Brand and marketing are important parts of your developer and landlord toolkit for future growth. Armed with the Build a Brand model, you can make sure you hone your skills in this area and maintain the edge over your competitors.

With the Build a Brand model under your belt and your ideal customer attracted to your co-living HMOs, it's now time to move on to the next step of the SPACES model: building your co-living HMOs' all-important community.

COMMUNITY LIVING

When you think about co-living, one of the first things that needs to spring to mind is community. Co-living HMOs have evolved out of people's need for urban living that provides a social support network and experience.

It is true that traditional HMOs can form communities. The friends I made while living in HMOs in Brighton when I was younger are friends for life. We formed a social circle and bond based on our experience of living together. The big difference with traditional HMOs is that the spaces were not specifically designed to enhance community, and there was no facilitation or support to help grow the community aspect. We were on our own and doing our own thing.

There are two key parts to a co-living HMO community: the community spaces themselves and the services you provide to nurture the community. Getting this first part right creates the optimum environment to encourage people to come together. Once you have created a co-living HMO space, you need to proactively support, facilitate and grow the community.

To get one step ahead, retain your housemates and supercharge your occupancy, you need to think differently. Using the methods described in Chapter 10, which covers the Space Design Blueprint, you will be able to create spaces that drive longer occupancy and better usability. In this chapter, we will discuss community managers, community events and partnerships, and interconnected communities; community onboarding and how to find the right housemates; and multi-generational living.

The role of community managers

If you are looking to grow and nurture a co-living HMO community, you need people in a role that encompasses more than standard lettings management. Whether you call this role 'manager' or 'facilitator', the important thing is that it reflects customer need.

Traditional HMOs were all about filling rooms, legal compliance and maintenance. These things are important, but times have changed and we as landlords are moving towards a concierge-style service to facilitate the community.

Unlike traditional letting agents, community managers are proactively driving an events schedule and initiatives to help build the community ethos. In this section, we will talk about how community managers organise events, partnerships and interconnected communities.

Community events and partnerships

A huge benefit of having a community manager in-house is that they can do things most letting agents are unable to do, such as running events and initiatives. These are great ways to bring people together to form bonds and friendships. One of the best ways to do this is by encouraging the housemates to eat and socialise together.

Co-Living Spaces' community managers organise localised events utilising the social spaces we covered in Chapter 10. There are a whole range of events your community manager can host for your co-living HMO communities.

You could add some competition into the process where housemates from different co-living HMOs can win a free evening meal for everyone. On Halloween, for example, the housemates carve pumpkins and send you images; the winning house then receives Deliveroo vouchers for the housemates' favourite takeaway. Other popular events are pizza nights, board games and the use of outdoor spaces for barbecues in the summer.

Another area where your manager can help promote community is through partnerships. Here, local gyms, personal trainers, running clubs, yoga clubs, cycle clubs etc provide discounts to your customers so they can work out together. Setting up and managing these partnerships is part of the manager's role in growing the community.

Interconnected and shared-interest communities

When customers become housemates and join the community, they are now your brand customers. If you are delivering a great customer journey, they will want to stay with the brand when they decide to move on, perhaps because they want a different location, a larger room, access to facilities such as co-working, or simply a change of scene. Community managers make it easy and seamless for customers to move around within the wider co-living community.

Many of my company's housemates have been with us for years, and have recommended us to their friends and colleagues. Our portfolio covers co-living HMOs, self-service hotels, commercial and self-contained flats so we can accommodate all stages of the customer lifecycle. If the customer is happy with your brand, they will always approach you first to see if you have anything suitable when their needs change.

Across your co-living HMO properties, you are likely to have a range of tenant types, including freelancers, entrepreneurs, digital nomads, tradespeople, account managers, office workers, shop workers, creatives, project managers and everything in between. These tenants have varied interests such as sport, travel, nature, design, painting, socialising, eating out, movie nights, programming, technology – the list is endless. The technology exists now to allow customers to choose a property based on the interests of the people already within that space, which is pretty cool. It will be interesting to see how tech such as this will create more niche co-living HMOs in the future. However, diverse groups have many benefits too. If you want people to collaborate together, diversity has a big role to play.

Miguel

Community onboarding

These days, technology plays a huge role in lettings. For your co-living HMOs, embrace technology to create a paperless experience with a mobile-first journey from viewing and onboarding through to events and management.

Having a good onboarding process is key to helping new housemates integrate into your co-living HMO community so they can familiarise themselves with all it has to offer. Once you have a process in place, it can be systemised and repeated by your community manager. The important thing to remember here is that the onboarding process starts long before the potential housemate enters the community; it begins with all the digital touchpoints they will encounter leading up to the check in.

Here are some elements to include in your onboarding process:

- Key tenancy information
- Overview of facilities such as barbecue zones, co-working, cinema rooms etc
- Introduction to other housemates
- The role of community managers and key contact details
- House rules and how to report any issues
- Any upcoming events
- Top tips on the area including where the nearest supermarkets, takeaways or deals are
- Gym and health recommendations
- Tour of the co-living HMO
- Welcome pack in the room

Find the right housemates

When landlords are designing the end-to-end customer experience, from selection and onboarding through to management and community, one question that comes up regularly is how to find the right housemates. This five stage process is something my company, Co-Living Spaces, has refined over the years based on experience, and follows religiously on every new application.

When you want to get someone in quickly, it can be tempting to jump a stage of the process, but each one is there for a reason so I urge you to resist this temptation. It is difficult to get the wrong person out of your co-living HMO and you might end up with other housemates leaving instead.

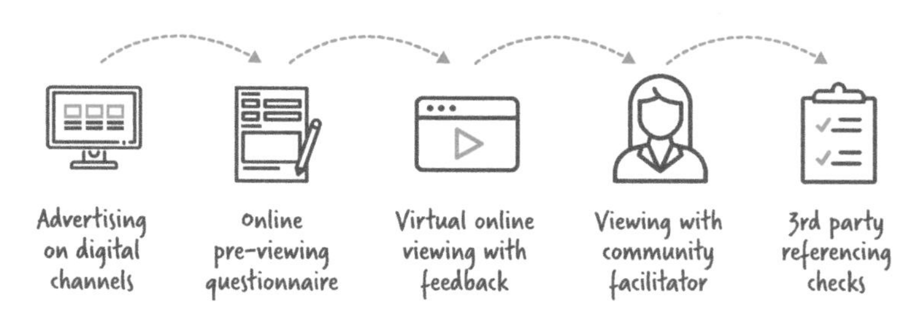

Multi-generational living

You may think that co-living HMOs are specifically for Millennials and Generation Z, those tech-savvy professionals with their on-demand lifestyle. While it is true that Millennials make up a large part of the community, there is a wider demographic. I have found that Generation X is also interested in being part of a co-living community.

One thing to consider is that the way people work is changing. Many of your housemates will be moving to a more flexible model, working full time or several days from home. This is why dedicated co-working spaces and project stations are so important across your portfolio.

CES

With a wide demographic comes a certain level of intergenerational living. Some spaces appeal mainly to Generation Z and Millennials, while others tend to see a mix of older Millennials and Generation X. My company has experimented with this for some time and the feedback has been positive. Perhaps surprisingly, we have seen a strong demand for co-living from people in Generation X who may be single, divorced or new to the area.

Whether you mix demographics or create niche properties, your co-living HMOs will attract a wide age range compared to traditional HMOs.

Summary

Enabling and nurturing communities is at the heart of co-living HMOs. You can achieve true community living for your customers through the physical spaces you design using the Space Design Blueprint and the service layer you provide on top. A focus on community and experience will increase your long-term occupancy.

In this chapter, we covered the role of community managers to help nurture a co-living community, organise events and brand partnerships for housemates, and coordinate interconnected communities across your brand. We examined how to find and onboard the right housemates, finishing off by touching on intergenerational living and how the different generations are embracing the idea of co-living HMOs.

With the concept of community living front of mind, I am sure you can see how the customer experience is more important in your co-living HMOs now than ever before. That is exactly what we are going to cover in the next step of the SPACES model.

Find out how experienced landlord Ajaz has been upgrading his existing portfolio into co-living HMOs to help nurture a community. What worked for him over the last fifteen years no longer works as competitors move into the market, causing occupancy issues. Not only has Ajaz future-proofed his portfolio and maximised his occupancy, he is also achieving much higher rents than before as housemates are happy to pay for a good-quality product.

To watch the full video visit
www.theco-livingrevolution.co.uk/mastermind

EXPERIENCE

Creating a great customer experience is more important now than ever before. Customers have the power, not the seller; the customer can vote with their feet and choose another co-living HMO product if the experience in your offering is not up to scratch. You will spend a lot of money developing your co-living spaces, so you need to ensure demand and occupancy.

This chapter, the fifth step of the SPACES model, will cover how to get your customer experience right. We will look at the need to choose your property management wisely. If your agency is doing a bad job, your customer satisfaction will be low and your churn will be high ('churn' refers to the number and frequency of customers moving out). You need to analyse your churn to understand why people are leaving as this will help you identify any problems.

Providing an amazing customer experience is a great way to differentiate yourself from your competitors. Customers will no longer compare your co-living HMO on price and finish, but on service, so you need to think of customer experience as part of your overall brand experience. Your ability to delight the customer at every stage of their co-living journey will be a game changer.

Improve the customer journey

To understand your customer experience, you need to get into the mindset of your customer, which involves understanding their whole journey. Let's look at an example of what this means.

CASE STUDY

Jane's Journey

Jane is a potential customer. She is thinking of renting a room in a co-living HMO property and she searches on SpareRoom. She sees a property she likes on SpareRoom and messages the agent.

Some toing and froing leads to a viewing. In the meantime, Jane has visited the website and social channels of the company managing the property to find out more. Jane visits the property to look around, after which she indicates she will take the room.

The agent starts the referencing process online, after which Jane and the landlord sign documentation and arrange move-in dates. Upon arrival, Jane is met by the agent who hands over the keys and shows her where things are in the house.

Jane moves in and loves her new room. The agent provides a phone number and email to report any problems. There is a leak from the en-suite toilet and Jane calls the agent, who organises a tradesperson to come out. There is ongoing communication between the agent and Jane until the leak is fixed.

The important takeaway here is that customer experience is not exclusively the product, but the whole journey. This encompasses brand, marketing, product, communication and service. The experience is how the space and service make your customer feel.

Co-living operations and management

Early on in my property journey, I realised that some letting agents offer a poor service, both to the landlord and the tenant. I have lost track of how many times tenants have recalled stories of agents ignoring them, not fixing issues or generally giving bad customer service.

The question of how to manage your co-living HMO portfolio depends on whether you are looking for a passive income or to get more involved. The reason I set up my own co-living HMO management company was to ensure my customers receive an amazing end-to-end journey. There is no point creating a great product if the after sales experience is bad. Focus on providing a great experience that delivers beyond the customers' expectation.

If you are looking for an operator company to provide management for your co-living HMOs, I would suggest you do some local research. Look for agents who are aligned with your goals of growing a community and treating your tenants as customers. If you can find a company to run the operations side the way you want it run, this will give you a more passive investment. Typically, an operator will take a percentage fee for management, plus a tenant find fee whenever people move out.

If you want a more active role in your investment, can you do your own management? The answer is yes, but if you are short of time, it may not be for you. You will need a list of both out-of-hours and in-hours tradespeople to fix issues, not to mention the legislation and certificates you have to keep on top of to ensure nothing runs out.

This may seem like a lot of work, but technology can help you to systemise processes. The real time-consuming areas are marketing, communications and viewings. You will sometimes get people not showing up for viewings, which is frustrating given the other demands on your time.

If you do want to explore managing your portfolio yourself, I would recommend you hire a part-time community manager working on a flexible freelance basis so that you can spend your time on finding and funding more deals. When I look at new locations to invest in, part of my decision-making process involves finding out what letting agents are in the area. If you are going to scale your portfolio, you need to know you have an agent on the ground who can grow with you.

Use technology to improve the experience

Technology has made its way into our everyday lives. If you identify the right technology to improve the customer journey, you will enhance their satisfaction. Co-living HMOs are a product designed around changing customer needs, so technology will play a part.

We have discussed the role of smart technology such as heating, mood lighting and mesh wi-fi in co-living HMOs. In the context of the customer experience, apps on the customer's smartphone are bridging the divide between the usability and management of the space. Many cloud-based property management systems come with dedicated housemate apps that allow the customer to engage with the brand and community quickly and efficiently via their digital devices. They can report any issues, access their tenancy documents, find out about discounts, sign up for additional services like room cleaning and communicate with the community manager. What was once a complicated raft of separate communications is now centralised and driven by technology.

Technology uses data in clever ways to make the customer journey seamless. No longer are housemates expected to fill out paper forms; everything is integrated at a click of a button. Sequences of events happen automatically and all the risk of human error is removed. Over the years, I have seen first-hand how technology can solve the most complex problems. By utilising technology, you can systemise your business, and in doing so make your customers' lives easier.

PROVIDE A GREAT END-TO-END CUSTOMER EXPERIENCE

THE CO-LIVING REVOLUTION™

Co-living HMO room rates

How much can you charge for rooms to ensure they sell? Over my years of managing my own portfolio, I have seen first-hand how pricing works to fill rooms all year round.

When planning your co-living HMO, you will want to get a sense of the correct pricing per room. To stack the deal initially, do some competitor analysis on SpareRoom and set a slightly lower figure based on examples of decent-quality rooms nearby. If you follow the advice in this book, you will have the best rooms available on the market and will be able to exceed these initial numbers, but it's a good way to stress test a deal, then over-perform upon launch.

I tend to group room pricing into one of three categories: low (sub 10 sqm), mid (10–14 sqm) and high (15+ sqm). When you're considering your pricing, you will also need to factor in if the room comes with a private bathroom as this will affect the overall price you can achieve.

At Co-Living Spaces, we use an approach called dynamic pricing which is based on our experience of owning and managing boutique aparthotels. In our hotels, we have a summer rate and a winter rate. This means we can rent our rooms out for more in the summer as there is more demand, whereas in the winter, there are fewer customers so our rates need to be competitive. In other words, we decrease and increase the prices in line with what is happening in the market, over-performing in the summer so we can be more competitive in the winter. You can apply the same concept to changes in the market that affect the rents you can charge in your co-living HMOs.

Enquiries from couples

As you advertise your co-living HMO, you may be approached by couples looking for rooms. Just like singles, couples are attracted to the combination of social lifestyle and value for money that co-living HMOs offer.

The important thing here is that you will have an HMO licence for not only a certain number of rooms, but also a certain number of people in the building. If you are operating a six-bedroom HMO licensed for six people in a non-Article 4 area, then you cannot accept any couples without further planning permission as this would push you into the sui generis bracket. If you own a five-bedroom HMO in the same area, then you can license it for six people without needing any further planning permission.

Given the number of enquiries my company has had from couples, there is a largely untapped opportunity to offer rooms to this part of the market. If you rent a room to a couple, you can ask a much higher amount for that room, but you will need to make sure that the kitchen and facilities meet the HMO planning requirements for the number of people. Speak to your architect or planning consultant about this.

Understand customer churn to increase occupancy

It is perfectly natural that your housemates will leave from time to time. As there are a number of reasons why people move on, the important thing is to gather data on their reason for leaving. Millennials and Generation Z may be changing jobs regularly as they make their way up the career ladder. The most common reasons I see for people moving on are new jobs in a different city, travelling and moving in with a partner.

Churn could also be due to issues you may not be aware of, from antisocial housemates and noise to room sizes, lack of storage, maintenance or the service you provide. This feedback is immensely valuable – if you don't know about an issue, then you can't fix it. Identifying issues early will enable you to reduce churn and boost your occupancy levels.

Once you understand your customer churn, the next area to focus on is how to promote customer longevity. There is no point working hard to sell new rooms if your existing customers are leaving. The key is to provide an amazing experience for your existing customers to retain them for the long term.

The first room your customer lives in is just the start of their journey; they may live in several other rooms, properties and apartments under your brand. The objective here is to encourage customers to move around within your interconnected communities and across your range of accommodation types for many years, so you need to think beyond the initial transaction and focus on the longevity of the relationship with your customers. The chances are many of your competitors will not be focusing on longevity and will be continually fighting to fill rooms. For every happy customer you retain for the long term comes the added bonus of them referring your brand to their friends and colleagues.

Summary

Happy customers stay with your brand and become advocates, forming an extension of your sales team and helping you maximise referrals and occupancy. Advocacy is when your customers become your fans, and it is the Holy Grail of marketing. Sounds good, eh?

To create advocates, you need to focus on designing a great customer experience as well as a great product. Using the approaches we have discussed in this chapter, which include how to visualise your customer journey, deciding on a suitable HMO management company, using technology to transform the customer experience, the role of room pricing and the importance of understanding customer churn, you will be able to deliver this great experience.

We are now nearly at the end of the SPACES model. There is only one step left to cover: how to scale your co-living HMO business.

Bonus Content

Visit **www.theco-livingrevolution.co.uk/bonus**
for your free content, checklists and resources to help you get started on your co-living HMO journey.

SCALE

Eventually, you will move from working on a single co-living HMO to multiple projects running concurrently every year. While you can do everything to start with, you will require a team around you to deliver the projects as you scale your business up.

Once you have delivered your first co-living HMO product to market and gathered initial feedback, you are then in a position to roll out a portfolio of similar projects. You can expand beyond your geographical area, but this requires you going back to the strategy stage to research your new target areas, power team, customer insight and numbers. Every subsequent project you deliver in your target area(s) can leverage the previous ones as you will already have a build specification, design guide and blueprint. Once you have done the hard work, it's time to scale your business and build a high-yielding portfolio to achieve financial freedom.

Systems and processes to scale your business

As you grow your business, your need for systemisation increases. In this section, we will cover some of the areas you need to consider as part of your business systemisation.

Strategic and financial

As your business expands, you will need to model financials, future cash-flow forecasts and business growth. I use the Google suite of products and Xero for all my company's financial spreadsheets and documents. Google Sheets and Google Docs are similar to Excel and Word with the ability to import and export Microsoft files.

Creating your own forecast is a good way to model any dips in your cash flow between your co-living HMO projects and investor repayments.

Operations

I would recommend moving all of your file management away from your desktop and into the cloud, both for back up and to become paperless.

I use Google Drive for this purpose. If one of your computers goes down (we have all been there!), you can be up and running on another computer within a short period of time. Regardless of your location, you can access all of your files. Centralising your spreadsheets in this way will help simplify your company operations.

Project delivery

At Co-Living Spaces, we use a task-management system called Asana to make sure all freelancers and employees are working efficiently from the same plan. Every Monday, I schedule tasks for the week ahead so that everyone knows what to work on.

Asana is designed to be used by teams to deliver projects and capture all communication around tasks, and the accompanying app is useful for brain dumping ideas as you think of them. Digitising all your task management will help give you clarity on project progress and communication.

The goal is to move any communication via email to a conversation thread against the relevant task on the software. This eliminates the need to search for conversations within your email to find out how a task is developing. It will save you a lot of grey hairs as you expand your co-living HMO business.

Management

In my co-living HMO management company, we have integrated property management software (PMS) to systemise the management side. This technology-first approach has allowed us to capture all customer information, documentation and communication along with compliance, reminders and financials in a single cloud-based location.

There is a whole range of PMS available. I would recommend shortlisting three software options and running a trial to compare. Visit the free bonus content at the end of the chapter for recommended PMS.

Processes

When you build a team, you will need to put some simple step-by-step processes in place to maintain consistency. Document the steps you take to do a task yourself, such as marketing properties, onboarding new customers, property management, community facilitating and exit, capture them online, and then use this to train your team or freelancers.

Your ability to document processes will allow you to outsource tasks to others and systemise your property business over time. It will also ensure ease of handover to new staff.

Marketing

Part of the Build a Brand model covers the marketing assets you will generate such as brand identity, social media, websites, branded PDFs and promotional content. It's important to back up all of your marketing assets to the cloud so that freelancers can access them for ongoing work. As your business grows, you will build up a network of trusted freelancers and small agencies to work on your brand, printed materials and digital assets.

To streamline your marketing, you will need to invest in a customer relationship management (CRM) system. This is a piece of software that organises all your contacts, allowing you to categorise them, store key information and set reminders to follow up. CRMs work particularly well for investor and networking leads.

This might seem like a lot of systems, but you make the changes step by step as you evolve, adding systems and processes as you require them. In other words, you learn how to do something manually, then replace it with a system. Technology is there to help us all gain more time to focus on the strategic things in our businesses.

Expand your team as you grow

As you scale up your business, you will need some help with your co-living HMO portfolio to deliver your product. After helping build two companies, I wanted a lean and agile team that tapped into changing work habits, so I created a home office with access to co-working space for workshops when needed. Rather than being tied to a single location, everyone involved has a healthy work-life balance as flexible hours are designed to fit around family life.

My team is a mixture of freelancers and part-time staff working on a semi-remote basis. We meet once a week for a team catch up and strategy session, then speak daily on both Asana and Zoom. If you take this approach, it will keep your overheads low and your team flexible. There are a lot of skilled people out there looking to work a few days per week on a flexible basis.

Empower your team

Your growing team will be looking to you for guidance and support, and you are likely to find yourself spending more time managing people than doing the thing you went into business for. One of the best ways to address this is to focus on finding the right people for your team, which means those who align with your mission and values. Once you have the right people, you can make better use of everyone's time by using technology to design systems they can follow.

No matter how busy you are, never skip a thorough onboarding process with new team members. It is important to allow them to spend a day or two getting to know the company, understanding the mission, seeing the co-living HMO products first-hand, meeting the team and logging into all the systems.

Your key role as a leader is to inspire, nurture and grow the team. You are responsible for the strategy and direction of the business. You set the mission, the purpose and the values that everyone is striving for. As a leader, you allocate the framework, support and time for innovation.

Innovation comes from the top down and requires you to champion its importance to the wider company mission, so don't be afraid to roll up your sleeves, get stuck in and lead by example.

Create a product-delivery blueprint

Congratulations! Delivering your first co-living HMO is the hard part. You are now in the position to create a guide to roll out all future projects.

Once you have completed your first co-living HMO fit out and have the blueprint for your product, you can replicate your success. At this stage, it is useful to create templates and checklists based on your first project to leverage the learnings. With each project you deliver, it is good practice to review and update the templates. For example, if during one project you forgot to add a small detail to the SOW that became a chargeable extra, you can make a note of it in your template for future projects.

Here is a list of templates, checklists and guides you can create to roll out your product for future co-living projects:

- Template SOW
- Template design appendix
- List of key suppliers and products
- Checklists for project setup
- Master project financials and costs spreadsheet
- Checklists for pre-launch
- Fit-out guide
- Paint colour guide

Summary

As you scale your business, you need to systemise and put processes in place for your team to follow, allowing you to focus on strategic growth and a pipeline of new projects. Utilising technology to centralise all information and communication will make your business more efficient and enable you to gain some strategic time.

A semi-remote team and a support network of professionals who can help deliver your goals will keep your business lean and agile. Your responsibility will be to lead and inspire the team so that everyone is heading in the right direction.

Creating your own product-delivery blueprint will allow you to roll out your co-living HMOs at scale, refining the blueprint as you go. One of the goals in Michael E Gerber's excellent book *The E-myth Revisited*[25] is to work on your business rather than in it. This is where technology and systemisation can work brilliantly to free up you time.

Bonus Content

Visit **www.theco-livingrevolution.co.uk/bonus**
for your free content, checklists and resources to help you get started on your co-living HMO journey.

Find out how David leapfrogged into the property industry after a successful army career by leveraging the knowledge, templates, product suppliers and systems provided on The Co-Living Mastermind™. David shares the confidence that he has gained from building out his own co-living HMO business.

To watch the full video visit
www.theco-livingrevolution.co.uk/mastermind

CONCLUSION — WHAT'S NEXT ?

The last decade has seen a huge shift in the evolution of the HMO. As investors and developers, we always need to have one eye on the future to spot emerging customer trends. Our co-living HMOs will evolve and adapt with every project. Only by continually moving forward will we be able to stay ahead of the curve.

With that in mind, let's have a look at…

The future of co-living

In this section, I will highlight the trends my company is following and experimenting with.

Co-living villages

Most people think of co-living as rented rooms with access to shared facilities such as kitchen, dining, lounge and garden, but co-living in the future will take place in hybrid developments that blend commercial and public spaces with rooms and self-contained apartments in a single large community. These urban villages will have their own ecosystem of services such as gyms, cafés, co-working, crèche and retail. The traditional co-living community may evolve to encourage wider local community use of general public spaces.

Flexible contracts and membership

The lines between short and long stay will blur as co-living becomes more service based. Traditionally, it's hotels and serviced accommodation that are short stay, starting from only a single night with linen changeover. Legislation in the future may provide more flexibility, allowing co-living customers to choose any length of stay, blurring the line between the hotel and co-living HMO experience.

Co-living for all life stages

Property brands will move towards a range of accommodation for all life stages with the focus on customer retention rather than just filling rooms. Customers will be able to move seamlessly between co-living HMOs, studios, apartments and houses under the same brand at a click of a button.

Energy-efficient buildings

By 2025, all rental properties will have to meet a minimum energy performance certificate (EPC) rating of C,[26] so landlords will need to develop or upgrade their properties with sufficient insulation and energy measures to hit these new targets. My company works closely with architects and an EPC assessor to maximise our energy efficiency across the portfolio each year.

As we move further into the future, landlords will need to integrate a range of renewable energy generation and storage facilities into their developments. Advancements in solar thermal, photovoltaics, heat pumps and heat recovery will create a host of new technologies that will help us build co-living HMOs that are sustainable, highly efficient and cheap to run.

Flexible live-work

Many companies now utilise technology and remote working, in some cases downscaling their office space. Offices may become small brand hubs for team building, meetings and workshops. Employees will have the option of semi-remote working from home or in co-working or public spaces.

A blend of co-working, workstations, breakout spaces and superfast wi-fi in your co-living HMOs means you are adapting to customer needs. You are no longer providing just accommodation; you are creating flexible live-work spaces.

Connectivity

Co-living HMO customers will require higher data speeds and connectivity to power their lifestyle through business-grade internet. They are likely to perform speed checks as part of their viewings to assess the suitability of the location. You will need the maximum data speed available to ensure there are no wi-fi blackspots, so invest in mesh technology for 100% signal coverage across the building.

The value of space

When deciding where to live, customers will require space for their flexible working arrangements, and co-living HMOs that can accommodate them will rent quickly and for the long term. There will be a trend towards large bedrooms with extra storage and integrated workstations. Rather than a large single open-plan social space, we may see a selection of community spaces.

Customers are also likely to prioritise health as part of their selection process. Exterior spaces that are well designed will enhance the overall co-living HMO experience and help improve mental health and wellbeing for customers.

Invest in your knowledge

The toolkit used by developers and landlords is changing rapidly with an emphasis on a high-yielding strategy, product design and brand experience. Those who invest in their knowledge of these skills will future-proof their portfolio, lead the field and make the biggest gains with both customer experience and financial returns.

Utilise the advice in this book to outperform your market and make sure you're continually looking for opportunities to learn. This is where a good mentor is a wise investment. Property is one big journey and your progress is directly affected by the knowledge you gain, the support you receive and the people you surround yourself with. Fast track your property journey by finding a mentor who is already creating the product and strategy you wish to create and leverage their knowledge.

It's important to remember that we are all learning every day and each new project will bring fresh opportunities. If you build a company that continues to act like a startup, it will never stand still, becoming more fulfilling and successful as a result. Startups listen to their customers and can innovate rapidly by remaining agile. It's too easy to lose this sense of innovation as your company grows and expands into the future.

Here is a list of ways your company can act like a startup every day:

- Remain clear on your mission and purpose
- Maintain your curiosity
- Strive to understand everything about your customer
- Nurture creativity within your environment and people
- Adapt and be willing to pivot if necessary
- Test new ideas and launch them quickly to market

The playing field is changing for HMOs. Now more than ever, it is important to ensure you have the edge using the techniques described in this book.

Do you want to be a Blackberry or an Apple? Blackberry did not keep up with the market or adapt quickly enough to change once Apple disrupted the industry, so it fell behind and customers voted with their feet.[27] Blockbuster Video did not adapt to changing buying habits and soon found itself pushed out of business by startups such as Netflix.[28] Change will always happen and the HMO market is no different. The important thing is how you deal with these changes.

Don't become a Blackberry or a Blockbuster. Now is the time to look to the future and invest in your knowledge and development so you can embrace change.

JOIN US ON THE CO-LIVING HMO DISCOVERY DAY

The Co-Living HMO Discovery Day is our interactive one-day event hosted several times a year. It provides an introduction to design-led Co-Living HMOs so that by the end of the training you know if this is the strategy for you. We have trained hundreds of landlords across the world with this full day of property education.

On the day we cover:

- How to create high yielding HMOs that replace your income
- How to start searching for suitable properties for conversion
- How to optimise space and design a great product
- How to build and nurture a community with a focus on experience

To find out more visit
www.theco-livingrevolution.co.uk

JOIN US ON THE CO-LIVING MASTERMIND ™

I have referred to our mastermind throughout this book and I would like to take the opportunity to introduce you to our core programme, The Co-Living Mastermind™.

If you would like help to achieve your goals, and are inspired to create properties similar to those in this book, then invest in yourself and join us on The Co-Living Mastermind™. This is the top level of Co-Living HMO training available in the UK, rated 9.4/10 by our mentees, which I deliver personally.

The Co-Living Mastermind™ is a mentoring programme for landlords and investors, where I work closely to provide support. The mastermind is designed both for new landlords looking to replace their income, and for existing landlords looking to future-proof their portfolios. We work with landlords across the UK and internationally to provide the knowledge, support, environment and accountability you need to get results.

We cover all levels of property development from smaller C3-C4 Co-Living HMO's through to larger Sui Generis 7+ bedroom Co-Living HMOs and mixed-use commercial conversion schemes.

The training goes into detail on all stages of your journey including:

- How to find the best sites suitable for Co-Living HMO's
- How to confidently stack and assess new leads
- How to add maximum value to your projects to recycle more funds
- Space design masterclasses to design the best product
- How to create schedules of work and successfully manage renovations
- How to launch your own property brand

What's included in The Co-Living Mastermind™:

- **Monthly Full Day Workshops** – sharing the latest practical techniques, step-by-step guides, space design masterclasses, residential and commercial cases studies to enable you to create your own Co-Living HMOs.
- **Monthly Deal Clinics** – giving you practical support to review sites you have found and help you assess to see if the deal stacks.
- **Private Mastermind WhatsApp Group** – for community and accountability.
- **Product and Supplier Design Guide** – access our key suppliers and products used to create your own Co-Living spaces, similar to our photoshoots shared in this book.
- **Power Team** – we share key contacts and recommendations.
- **Exclusive Site Visit** – see behind the scenes at one of our projects to get up close to the latest design and build techniques.

To find out more and setup a 1-2-1 strategy call visit:
www.theco-livingrevolution.co.uk/mastermind

THE CO-LIVING MASTERMIND™

REFERENCES

1. www.theatlantic.com/business/archive/2016/09/millennial-housing-communal-living-middle-ages/501467
2. Hester, J 'A brief history of co-living spaces' (Bloomberg CityLab, 2016) www.bloomberg.com/news/articles/2016-02-22/a-brief-history-of-co-living-spaces-from-19th-century-boarding-houses-to-millennial-compounds
3. Reeder, J 'Hacking home: Coliving reinvents the commune for a networked age (Sharable, 2012) www.shareable.net/hacking-home-coliving-reinvents-the-commune-for-a-networked-age
4. www.common.com
5. www.habyt.com
6. www.thecollective.com
7. https://bungalow.com
8. https://cohabs.com
9. https://livezoku.com
10. Hu, T, 'Co-living picks up speed in Asia' (JLL, 2018) www.joneslanglasalle.com.cn/en/newsroom/co-living-picks-up-speed-in-asia; https://vipproperty.com/residential-co-living-trend-accelerates-in-asia; JLL, 'How co-living is filling a need in Asia' (JLL 2019) www.joneslanglasalle.com.cn/en/trends-and-insights/cities/how-co-living-is-filling-a-need-in-asia; PropertyInvestorToday, www.propertyinvestortoday.co.uk; Elvinvest, 'The impact of co-living in Europe (Elvinvest) https://elvinvest.ch/the-impact-of-co-living-in-europe
11. Housing Act 1985, section 345 (Legislation.gov. Retrieved 30 March 2015) www.legislation.gov.uk/ukpga/1985/68/section/345/1991-02-01?timeline=true
12. Private renting (Gov.uk) www.gov.uk/private-renting/houses-in-multiple-occupation
13. Built Asset Management 'New data shows 312% increase in renters ditching single accommodation in favour of co-living' (BAM, 2020) https://builtassetmanagement.co.uk/new-data-shows-312-increase-in-renters-ditching-single-accommodation-in-favour-of-co-living
14. Bahirat, T, Design thinking is Apple's Success Mantra (Great Learning, 2020), www.mygreatlearning.com/blog/design-thinking-is-apples-success-mantra
15. Planning Portal website www.planningportal.co.uk
16. Ikea, One Shared House 2030 Survey (2019) http://onesharedhouse2030.com/results
17. This means all of your money invested in the deal has been returned ie a free property!

18 Fizzy Living www.fizzyliving.com

19 Moda Living wwww.modaliving.com

20 Kelley, T; Kelley, *D Creative Confidence: Unleashing the creative potential within us all* (Harper Collins, 2015

21 Ikea, One Shared House 2030 Survey (2019) http://onesharedhouse2030.com/results

22 Google, Zero Moment Of Truth (ZMOT) (Think With Google) www.thinkwithgoogle.com/marketing-strategies/micro-moments/zero-moment-truth

23 About Nike, https://about.nike.com

24 About LinkedIn, https://about.linkedin.com

25 Gerber, ME The *E-Myth Revisited: Why most small businesses don't work and what to do about it* (HarperBus, 2001)

26 Find an energy certificate (GOV.UK) www.gov.uk/find-energy-certificate

27 Ritchie, R 'How Apple killed Blackberry' (iMore, 2020) www.imore.com/how-apple-killed-blackberry

28 Newman, R 'How Netflix (and Blockbuster) killed Blockbuster' (US News, 2010) https://money.usnews.com/money/blogs/flowchart/2010/09/23/how-netflix-and-blockbuster-killed-blockbuster

THE CO-LIVING REVOLUTION™

THE CO-LIVING REVOLUTION™

THE CO-LIVING REVOLUTION™

ACKNOWLEDGEMENTS

First and foremost, I would like to thank my wonderful wife Melissa and my daughter Jasmine for their endless support during the years I have been working on the book. There have been a lot of late nights as I've put this together and I could not have done it without them.

I would like to thank Simon Zutshi for his help as I began my property journey many years ago, prototyping the early incarnations of co-living HMOs, and his ongoing support for me when I was launching my own mentoring programme. Simon's values of integrity and trust have shone through and he has been immensely generous with his time.

I would also like to thank Daniel Hill for his support over the years. He has helped me to plan strategically, put business systems in place and grow The Co-Living Revolution brand. Daniel has a phenomenal knowledge of business systems and it is a pleasure to spend time with him.

Finally, I would like to thank my good friend and business partner Carly Houston, with whom it is a privilege to work, be it launching boutique aparthotels through to development projects. Carly has always been true to her values and her work ethic is nothing short of exceptional.

THE AUTHOR

Stuart Scott is a renowned property developer, innovator and public speaker. He has helped build a number of successful award-winning businesses, including a creative agency and a product-design company. Prior to entering into property, he headed up innovation teams designing products and experiences for some of the world's biggest brands including Porsche, Microsoft, Gap, Nike, Tom Dixon and Penguin Random House.

Stuart decided to pivot away from his life as a busy company director to follow his passion for property full time and achieve a better work-life balance. He now uses his product design and innovation skills alongside property development to drive positive change in the shared-living market.

Stuart has many years' experience in delivering high-end refurbishments and complex commercial to residential developments. He has built a multi-million-pound portfolio in the South-East of England, combining co-living HMOs, boutique aparthotels, single lets and commercial spaces. He won the highly prestigious 2019 UK Property Developer of the Year and 2018 UK Property Investor of the Year for his work to pioneer change in the property market. He is a regular on the public speaking circuit where he educates people on high-yielding property, design thinking and innovation.

His development company Co-Living Spaces is on a mission to change the way people live together. Stuart now mentors other landlords on The Co-Living Mastermind™ to help them build their own co-living HMOs.

www.theco-livingrevolution.co.uk
www.co-livingspaces.co.uk
www.stuart-scott.co.uk

Lightning Source UK Ltd.
Milton Keynes UK
UKHW020229060722
405412UK00007B/181